Kathleen —

An interesting perspective —

Thompson & Juarez are old friends.

[signature]

04 - 25 - 2013

Tejanos in Gray

NUMBER NINE: FRONTERAS SERIES
Sponsored by Texas A&M International University

José Roberto Juárez, General Editor

A list of titles in this series is available at the end of the book.

Tejanos in Gray

Civil War Letters of Captains Joseph Rafael de la Garza and Manuel Yturri

Edited and with an Introduction by Jerry Thompson
Translations by José Roberto Juárez

Texas A&M University Press | College Station

This paper meets the requirements of ANSI/NISO Z39.48-1992
(Permanence of Paper).
Binding materials have been chosen for durability.

Library of Congress Cataloging-in-Publication Data
Garza, Joseph Rafael de la, 1838–1864.
[Correspondence. English. Selections]
Tejanos in gray : Civil War letters of Captains Joseph Rafael de La Garza
and Manuel Yturri / edited and with an introduction by Jerry Thompson ;
translations by José Roberto Juarez.
    p. cm. — (Fronteras series ; no. 9)
Includes bibliographical references and index.
ISBN-13: 978-1-60344-243-5 (cloth : alk. paper)
ISBN-10: 1-60344-243-X (cloth : alk. paper)
ISBN-13: 978-1-60344-268-8 (e-book)
ISBN-10: 1-60344-268-5 (e-book)
    1. Garza, Joseph Rafael de la, 1838–1864—Correspondence.
2. Yturri Castillo, Manuel—Correspondence. 3. Mexican American
soldiers—Texas—Correspondence. 4. Texas—History—Civil War,
1861–1865—Personal narratives. 5. United States—History—Civil War,
1861–1865—Personal narratives, Confederate. 6. Texas—History—Civil
War, 1861–1865—Participation, Mexican American—Sources. 7. United
States—History—Civil War, 1861–1865—Participation, Mexican
American—Sources. 8. Mexican Americans—Texas—History—19th
century—Sources. I. Thompson, Jerry D. II. Yturri Castillo, Manuel.
Correspondence. English. Selections. III. Title. IV. Series: Fronteras series ;
no. 9.
    E580.G37 2011
    973.7′8—dc22

                              2010034370

For Helen and John Yturri,
Sister and Brother,
and Heirs of a Proud Tejano Legacy

Contents

Illustrations

Translator's Note

Most of Manuel Yturri's letters were written in Spanish, while one-third of Joseph R. de la Garza's were in English; a few times Yturri began a letter in English or Spanish and then shifted to the other. Although Yturri wrote in both languages, it is evident that he preferred Spanish. When either man wrote in English, he rarely used contractions (with the exception of de la Garza's letter of July 31, 1863). Nevertheless, some contractions are used in the translation to provide a familiar tone and allow the letters to be read easily. In some instances I added punctuation for clarity, and some hastily constructed sentences are now divided into two or more. The scarcity of paper probably kept Yturri from paragraphing more often, but I have created paragraphs as it seemed appropriate for each writer. Occasionally I have added terms in brackets to clarify a passage. The use of numerals or words for numbers follow the originals. I have kept the original capitalization, punctuation, spelling, and abbreviations in the letters or sections they wrote in English.

The phrase "mi alma" can be translated in many ways. Since Yturri used "darling" and "dear" in the letters he wrote in English, I have used those two terms interchangeably for the Spanish. When translated simply as "the little girl," the phrase "la niña" sounds cold, so I have translated it as "our daughter." The phrase "amigos y amigas" is translated simply as "friends" rather than the cumbersome "male and female friends." Where I was not sure of the exact translation, I have placed endnotes to explain my usage. In a few instances ellipsis points are used when the text is torn or unreadable.

Sara Alicia Pompa assisted with the translation of the anonymous poem relating to de la Garza's death that appears in the appendix.

—JOSÉ ROBERTO JUÁREZ

Introduction

The contentious 1860–61 secession crisis and the bloody Civil War that followed were two of the most traumatic chapters in the long and tumultuous history of Texas. Before the bloody conflict had run its weary course, thousands of young Texans, many of them mere boys, lay dead on a hundred distant battlefields, from the rocky ridges of Pennsylvania and the gentle farmlands of Virginia to the snow-crowned mountains of New Mexico Territory. The war changed forever the lives of the men and women who lived through it, and effects of the struggle, both political and psychological, would profoundly and adversely influence the course of events in Texas and the nation for more than a century.

The exact number of Mexican Texans who served in the Civil War may never be known with certainty; sadly, even many of the names of the Tejanos who served have been lost. This historical omission is due primarily to the fact that relevant data, such as muster rolls and personnel records, especially those of soldiers who were in frontier militia units, have been lost, or in some instances were never compiled. To complicate the historical record, many of the recruiting and enrolling officers, as well as regimental clerks and adjutants, possessed little if any knowledge of Spanish. Consequently, Spanish-surnamed individuals had their names spelled phonetically and in several different ways. The fact that large numbers of Tejanos who enlisted in the Confederate and Union armies were illiterate also presented complications. Nevertheless, as many as 4,000 Spanish-surnamed individuals, who either volunteered or were drafted, participated in the war in one capacity or another.[1]

Two very literate and educated young men from San Antonio, Manuel Yturri y Castillo and Joseph Rafael de la Garza, became part of the epic struggle and left a set of rare and revealing personal letters. Yturri survived the war and lived into old age in the next century, while de la

Garza died at the age of twenty-six, leading his company in a charge against Federal lines at the bloody Battle of Mansfield during the 1864 Red River Campaign. Born during the early days of the infant Republic of Texas, both Yturri and de la Garza came of age in San Antonio during some of the most eventful years in the history of Texas. Manuel Yturri was born on March 19, 1838, and although a baptismal record has not been found, it appears that Joseph de la Garza was born at about the same time. Four years later Mexican general Rafael Vásquez rode north from the Rio Grande to raise the Mexican flag over the Alamo City. Seven months after that, on September 11, 1842, Gen. Adrián Woll led a second Mexican army into San Antonio. Although both Vásquez and Woll retreated across the Rio Grande, such events became legendary in the collective memory of San Antonio residents, as was the 1835 siege of Bexar and the bloody battle for the Alamo the following March; as evidence of the violence that had once engulfed the town, in 1912 a cannonball was found embedded in the walls of the de la Garza residence at what is today Houston Street and Main Avenue. By the time of the Civil War, San Antonio had become one of the most fought-over cities in North America. Both Yturri and de la Garza were descendants of proud Bexareño families with deep roots in the mesquite-infested and bloodied soil of South Texas.[2]

The Villa de San Fernando de Béxar was one of the oldest communities in Texas, having been chartered by Canary Islanders in 1731. The Yturri family was proud not only of their Isleño roots but also of their Basque ancestry. Manuel Yturri's father, Manuel Yturri y Castillo, had acquired an old gristmill that dated back to 1729 as well as a large piece of property near Mission Espada. With the secularization of the mission lands in 1824, he also came in possession of 160 acres of the former *labores* (fields) of Mission Concepción on the east of the San Antonio River and the Acequia de la Concepción. By this time the family had established a home just north of the Plaza de Armas, not far from the San Antonio River. A large rock-and-adobe home was later constructed at 327 South Presa Street. From a sprawling ranch complex, centered ten miles south of San Antonio, the Yturri family also kept one of the largest cattle herds in the area. Although the family loaned money and provided provisions to the Spanish Army, they maintained their influence and prominence in the years following Mexican independence.[3]

While the Yturri family struggled for land, wealth, and respectability, José Antonio de la Garza, Joseph Rafael de la Garza's father, acquired much of the land between the San Antonio River and Leon Creek and was said to be the largest landowner in Bexar County. He also owned land on the north side of the city at what is today Breckenridge Park and Alamo Heights. De la Garza also took pride in being the first in Texas to coin money and the first to use the Lone Star as an emblem. The family's "loyalty to Texas as a province of Spain, a state of Mexico, of the United States, and of the Southern Confederacy" inspired the Texas legislature to name a county on the Caprock in West Texas in their honor in 1876.[4]

Yet in the decades that followed Texas independence, the Yturri and de la Garza families came under tremendous stress. They watched as one of the Tejano leaders in the community, Juan Nepomuceno Seguín, a hero of the Texas Revolution, a mayor of San Antonio (1840–42), and the only Mexican Texan to serve in the senate of the republic, was forced to flee across the Rio Grande. In the years following the fall of the Alamo and the Battle of San Jacinto, outside forces came to dominate the economic and political life of San Antonio, a vibrant and thriving community that not only served as headquarters for the frontier army in Texas but also, with a population of 8,235 by 1860, had surpassed Galveston as the largest city in Texas.[5] By the time of the Civil War, German and English were as common a language on the streets of San Antonio as Spanish.

As part of the ranching and landholding Bexareño elite, the Yturri and de la Garza families did more than adjust to the ever-increasing influences of American expansionism, they prevailed. Whereas other Tejanos, especially those in the lower Rio Grande Valley, were dispossessed of their lands and joined Juan Nepomuceno Cortina in his historic and bloody 1859 revolt, the Yturri and de la Garza families prospered in

1. Carolina Angela de la Garza, sister of Joseph de la Garza, was married to Bartholomew Joseph DeWitt, a prominent frontier merchant, sutler, and one of the founders of San Angelo. Mother of five children, Carolina died unexpectedly in San Antonio in 1866, perhaps a victim of the cholera epidemic that swept the city. DeWitt first named the settlement of gambling houses, saloons, and trading posts on the North Concho River "Santa Angela," in honor of his deceased wife. The name was corrupted to "San Angela," and in 1883 federal officials changed the name of the small community to San Angelo. Courtesy of John and Helen Yturri.

2. This statue of Carolina Angela de la Garza DeWitt overlooks the North Concho River at the San Angelo Visitors Center, San Angelo, Texas. Photograph by Jerry Thompson.

a Texas that was increasingly dominated by Anglos. The social and economic standing of the two families in San Antonio was greatly enhanced by intermarriage and their ability to assimilate. Prior to the Civil War, for example, Joseph de la Garza's older sister, Margarita, married James L. Trueheart, a Virginia-born city alderman, while another older sister, Carolina, married Bart J. DeWitt, a prominent and influential trader and sutler. During this time, Manuel Yturri's younger sister, Vicenta, married Ernest B. Edmunds, a respected Louisiana merchant. In small part, intermarriage helps explain the Yturri and de la Garza tolerance of outsiders and their eventual tilt toward disunion. Unlike other prominent San Antonio Tejano families such as the Navarros and Seguíns, however, the Yturris and de la Garzas owned no slaves.[6]

Sons of respected San Antonio elite, Manuel Yturri and Joseph de la Garza were well educated and fluent in both Spanish and English. Like several of the sons of the city's other prominent Tejano families, de la Garza was educated at St. Joseph's College, a Jesuit school at Bardstown, in the bluegrass country of north-central Kentucky. There he studied the usual Greek and Latin classics along with theology. The second Jesuit rector of the college, John B. Emig, remarked in 1852 that de la Garza was a "good boy, very kind, polite and obedient to his teachers, very attentive to his Christian duties and very diligent in his collegiate studies." According to the rector, de la Garza was a young man of "fine disposition . . . very mild and cheerful, always in good humor and someone who had never uttered an improper word."[7] Yturri also attended St. Joseph's College but went on to the University of Pennsylvania in Philadelphia. On the eve of the Civil War, the Yturri and de la Garza families became united when Manuel Yturri married Elena de la Garza, Joseph's older sister and the seventh child of José Antonio de la Garza and María Josefa Menchaca.

In early 1861 both de la Garza and Yturri watched anxiously as the ever-deepening secession crisis engulfed San Antonio when zealous Texans coerced the Georgia-born and physically infirm Maj. Gen. David E. Twiggs, commander of the U.S. Army in Texas, into surrendering not only the arsenal there but also all Federal property and forces in his vast department. Yet there was also a pronounced Unionist sentiment in the city that emanated, in part, from its large German population. Partly due to their longstanding affection for Unionist standard-bearer Gov. Sam Houston, the Tejano community, including the Navarro, Seguín, de la Garza, Rodríguez, Ruiz, and Yturri families, also inclined toward Unionism and hesitated at the idea of secession. The "county and city is Union beyond doubt," the *Weekly Alamo Express* proclaimed in February 1861. But when the vote on secession came on March 2, Bexar County, which was also a hotbed for the Knights of the Golden Circle and men from the South (including the de la Garza and Yturri in-laws), approved secession by a vote of 827–709. When the locally recruited Alamo Rifles began to drill in the city, they were denounced as Black Republicans and Abolitionists, and the company commander was forced to issue a proclamation declaring that they were prepared to defend the state against Lincoln and his Republican rabble.[8] Seriously outnumbered, outmaneuvered, and realizing the gravity of the moment, a few Texans such as Houston remained defiant and attempted to forestall secession by proposing that the state return to its 1836–45 roots as an independent republic. But by the late spring of 1861, it was too late. Few listened to Houston's prophetic assertions that to join a Southern Confederacy would involve the state in a war that the South could not win. In time a majority of the Bexareño Tejanos came to embrace the spirit of rebellion. Texas not only pushed aside and then suppressed any opposition to secession but also plunged headfirst into the bloody cauldron of civil war.

With Texas joining the Confederate States of America, companies of zealous young men, frequently raised by local political leaders who often equipped the men at their own expense, began drilling in many towns and villages in the Lone Star State. Recruits came in the hundreds from the farms, ranches, and small villages "rarin' for a fight." Most expected a ninety-day war and assumed they would be home by the fall. Some realized that they were fighting against tremendous odds, but intoxicated by Southern pride and invigorated by the concept of states' rights, they were anxious to achieve fame in what they thought would be a glorious struggle. To most of the young men, going to war was idealized as a grand adventure. Everyone realized that they were on the crest of a floodtide of history.

Uniforms of the Rebel Texans varied greatly by style and color. A few of the officers, such as Yturri and de la Garza, could afford fancy gray uniforms, but many soldiers marched off to war in homespun butternut. Most young Rebels had wide-brimmed hats, while Tejanos from around San Antonio, the lower Nueces River, and the Rio Grande frontier preferred the sombrero. Of the almost ninety regiments recruited from Texas, two-thirds were cavalry, a very different makeup than in other states of the Confederacy. Going off to war on foot was less than honorable for many Texans, who had spent a large part of their life on horseback. Of the 92,145 males between the ages of eighteen and forty-five who were listed on the 1860 Texas census, approximately 70,000 or more would serve in the Confederate army or the state militia. Of this number perhaps as many as 5,000 deserted, and by the end of the war, thousands of others lay dead.

No one in 1861, including the youthful Yturri and de la Garza, had any idea of what lay ahead. Only a few of the older recruits were veterans of the Texas Revolution or the Mexican War and knew the taste of combat. Some Bexareños had fought Comanches on the frontier, but such campaigns rarely lasted for more than a few months. Most officers, including the two young Tejanos, both of whom rose to the rank of captain, had little knowledge of military tactics or even of how to drill their men. But they were tough men, brave to a fault, experienced riders, and capable shooters. In fact, Manuel Yturri had the reputation in San Antonio of being a superb marksman with either a rifle or a shotgun. Training camps were established at Brenham, Dallas, Waco, Harrisburg, Victoria, San Antonio, and near Houston. Here the young recruits were drilled endlessly, and when not drilling, the men overindulged in fiery orations or intoxicating spirits.

Most of the raw recruits, like Yturri and de la Garza, were in their late teens and early twenties, although men as old as sixty and boys as young as fourteen were not uncommon. Weapons and equipment varied greatly, and many were terribly antiquated. For example, three companies of the Sibley Brigade that drilled at San Antonio and marched off to conquer New Mexico Territory were equipped only with nine-foot-long lances. One young Texan recorded that his company was "armed with squirrel guns, bear guns, sportsman's guns, shotguns, both single and double barrel, in fact guns of all sorts." A few men had Colt revolvers, while others possessed only a Bowie knife. As the men and boys rode off to war, ladies, including those in San Antonio, presented them with colorful, carefully sewn flags.[9]

Joseph R. de la Garza enlisted in Capt. Samuel W. McAllister's Alamo Rifles on March 31, 1862, for three years or the duration of the war and was paid a bounty of fifty dollars. McAllister had no doubt that Texas was to be invaded, encouraging anyone desiring to enlist to rendezvous as soon as possible at either the Braden House or Staubbacker's Bar Room. Two months later the *San Antonio Semi-Weekly News* remarked that the city had never seen "such a spirit of patriotism" as that displayed by the Alamo Rifles, the "best army in the South." Moreover, the company was "warranted to shoot a Yankee at 1,000 yards." The Alamo Rifles would eventually become Company K, 6th Texas Infantry.[10]

At age twenty-four, Manuel Yturri also joined the Alamo Rifles as a private before reenlisting in Company H, 6th Texas Infantry as a first corporal. He then transferred to Col. James Duff's 33rd Texas Cavalry. A year later Yturri was elected second lieutenant in Col. Philip Nolan Luckett's 3rd Texas Infantry and then first lieutenant before being promoted to captain.[11]

Luckett was a Virginia-born physician who had settled at Corpus Christi. Elected to command the 3rd Texas Infantry, he was assigned to the Western Subdistrict of Texas, which included a number of scattered and isolated posts along the Rio Grande from Brownsville to Laredo. "Hordes of northern despots who have decreed our subjugation" were preparing to land on the Texas coast, Luckett told his men. "You will show what patriotism can do! I know that every chord in your bosom vibrates to your country's call," the colonel continued. "You have the proud position of defending the women and children of Western Texas from a ruthless invasion." Amazingly, both Yturri and de la Garza later managed to avoid the humiliating Confederate surrender at Arkansas Post, Arkansas, on January 11, 1863. Yturri was on leave at the time, while de la Garza was in Austin on detached service.[12]

Personal correspondence, diaries and journals, or other private documents of any kind relating to Tejanos during the war remain rare. A few scattered letters of Col. Santos Benavides, the highest-ranking Mexican Texan in the Confederate Army, survive in archives and private collections; de la Garza served under Benavides on the border in 1862. A few letters also survive by Capt. José Angel Navarro, a graduate of St. Vincent's College at Cape Girardeau, Missouri, who after studying law at Harvard returned to San Antonio, where he was elected three times to the Texas House of Representatives. Harvard's only Tejano to serve the Confederacy, he fled San Antonio for Mexico in November 1863 largely because of the prevailing racism and prejudice in the state at the time. Writing from San Fernando de Rosas, Coahuila, south of Eagle Pass, on December 1, 1863, Navarro informed Santiago Vidaurri, governor of Nuevo Leon and Coahuila, that he had arrived in Mexico "for the purpose of settling permanently." Knowing Vidaurri's sympathies for the Confederacy, the captain promised to explain his reasons for abandoning Texas. "It is enough to tell you," he wrote, "that I left because the military authorities in San Antonio treated me unjustly. This is in accord with my previous convictions and past experience that those of Mexican extraction do not enjoy in this country the same privileges as the natives."[13] Others were even more critical of the way Tejanos were treated in the state. Writing from Brazos Santiago, on the coast near Brownsville, shortly before the end of the war, Antonio Abad Dias, a fifty-year-old second lieutenant in the Union Army, could only recall with horror the crimes inflicted on Tejanos by Confederate authorities, especially after the controversial 1862 draft. The "horrible and animalistic acts," he wrote, were "not unlike a swarm of bees" and "boils the blood in your veins." Although Captains de la Garza and Yturri remained loyal to the Confederacy, friends and relatives, including de la Garza's older brother, Antonio, perhaps disillusioned by the death of his brother and hoping

3. Four San Antonio classmates proudly pose in this rare 1850s ambrotype. Manuel Yturri is seated second from left while one of the sons of José Antonio Navarro is thought to be on the far right. Courtesy of John and Helen Yturri.

to avoid conscription, rode south across the Rio Grande, where he took exile in Piedras Negras, Coahuila, across the river from Eagle Pass.[14]

Certainly the most valuable set of letters by Tejanos are those of Captains Yturri and de la Garza. Neither man was typical of the many Tejanos who served in the conflict. In contrast, the vast majority of Mexican Texans who joined the Confederate Army or enrolled in the militia tended to be poor, generally uneducated, frequently landless, and mostly from the Rio Grande frontier, the lower Nueces River, San Antonio, and the ranches around Goliad. The same was also true of the majority of Federal Tejano recruits, many of them recent immigrants from Mexico living in the lower Rio Grande Valley. Recruited by the Union Army in late 1863 and early 1864, many were desperately poor, second-rate citizens in a land that had once been theirs, and men who were lured by the promise of an enlistment bounty of as much as $300.[15]

How many of de la Garza's and Yturri's letters were lost during the war or in the years that followed is unknown; considering the frequency of Yturri's letters in 1864 and 1865, it appears certain that many of his earlier letters are indeed lost. Overall, however, the de la Garza and Yturri letters provide the historian with a wonderful window into a turbulent and uncertain time in the history of Texas and the South. Their correspondence not only reflects each man's deep affection for his family in San Antonio, but also a loneliness and desperation common among all soldiers at the time. After de la Garza fell at the bloody Battle of Mansfield and his brother-in-law Bart DeWitt brought his body back to San Antonio for burial, Yturri's letters continued and thus offer a glimpse into a broken and battered army and the breakup of the Trans-Mississippi Confederacy. He vividly portrays a hungry, barefooted, miserable, and disheartened soldiery who became increasingly disillusioned, especially after the surrender of Lee's Army of Northern Virginia at Appomattox Court House, Virginia, on April 9, 1865, and Gen. Joseph E. Johnston's capitulation at Durham Station, North Carolina, seventeen days later. The once-proud Texans in gray, beset with pain and desperation, devolved into a mob of mere marauders, some robbing and plundering their way home to the Lone Star State.

De la Garza's and Yturri's letters tell the story of two young men in the prime of their lives who were caught in the violent tide of history, men who performed their duty to the best of their ability in a war that grew increasingly unpopular and bloody. Yturri survived the cruel conflict and returned home to his family in San Antonio. There he helped raise a large family; became a city alderman, prominent rancher, and businessman; and lived to the age of seventy-five, dying after a long illness at the family home on South Presa Street on February 26, 1913.[16] By that time his brother-in-law Joseph Rafael de la Garza had been at rest in San Antonio's San Fernando Cemetery for forty-nine years.

—JERRY THOMPSON

Tejanos in Gray

Part 1

Letters of Capt. Joseph de la Garza

*"Don't worry about me. If you hear that they killed or wounded [me,]
tell them that it's okay, he died well."*

—JOSEPH DE LA GARZA,
OCTOBER 27, 1863

4. Capt. Joseph Rafael de la Garza was mortally wounded
at the Battle of Mansfield on April 8, 1864. Institute of Texan
Cultures, UTSA, 073-1145. Courtesy of Helen Yturri.

Camp H. E. McCulloch, Victoria
April 30, 1862

Dear Mother,

We all got here this morning in good health after having passed some days very tired, but taking everything into account, very happy.[1] The day we left San Antonio we camped on the Salado, then we covered 15 and 20 miles every day.[2] I endured the trip better than I thought. Now only the bottom of my feet hurt me a little. In two or three days I'll be refreshed enough to go to the city (which is some 4 to 5 miles distant) to take my picture and send it to you.

This morning we had a general inspection. There are more than 600 men. I believe that by the 10th of the coming month we will leave for Alleyton.[3] If you don't get this letter in your hands soon, send me your answer to that city. Eugenio [Navarro] is very well as is Pedro Ville [Sarats].[4] Tell Fermin that Pedro leaves for Goliad tomorrow.[5] Tell Manuel [Yturri] when he gets back to stay in San Antonio until the captain arrives, because I can assure you that he wouldn't like this place as much as he would there.

I'm already desirous of seeing all of you. It seems like a year since I last saw you. Tell my sisters, brothers and also Eugenio's [family], and the rest that I send them my most tender love. I hope this war ends quickly and God grant me life to see you again. I can assure you that one cannot be as comfortable as at one's home. But God is great and I hope we'll have better times.

I can't tell you anything about the camp right now because I know nothing about it. Tomorrow or day after tomorrow we'll begin to provide service. Up to now I don't think I would like a military career, but we'll see later. Right now I'm very comfortable sitting in my tent writing these few lines, but in a few days who knows?

Receive the tender love of
Your son,
Jos. R. Garza

May God preserve you.
I have more gray hair now than ever.
Camp Henry McCulloch
Victoria, Texas
Paper is very scarce.

———◆·▶◀·◆———

45 miles from Tyler, Tex.[6]
July 6 of 1862

My dear Mother,

Up to now I'm doing very well and comfortable. I've enjoyed good health. I had the pleasure of receiving a letter from Elena [Yturri] 4 or 5 days ago.[7] The poor [soul] tells me I frightened her excessively, but I did it without malice. I didn't know how Manuel was and in what way he had joined in that company, but now I do know the order is here and he can stay there. But he better not come close to this regiment because as soon as he does he will have to come join us.

In 3 or 4 days we'll enter Arkansas and I'll write you again. Take good care of yourself for with God's help I expect we'll see each other again in a short time and I would feel very badly if I were to find you in poor health. Don't live by yourself. Don't worry about your sons, we're already men. As soon as this business is solved, I'm going to bring Leonardo and in that way he won't wait for me alone, for my intention is to bring him before returning to San Antonio.[8] Many remembrances to my sisters and brothers, relatives and friends from me and Eugenio and Pedro. And you receive the heart of your son who desires to see you.

Jos. R. Garza
When you write me address the letters
in this manner:
Jos. R. Garza
Company K

6th Reg., Mt. Tex. Inftry.

Little Rock, Ark.[9]

Care of Capt. [Sam William]

McAllister[10]

Via Tyler, Tex.

Tell me how everybody is, my sisters and brothers and what they're doing, how they spend their time. How is the harvest from the La Espada field and really all that pertains to our family for I get very great pleasure when I get a letter. I even feel like I'm in your company.[11] Not having any more to say, I remain your caring and loving son.

Jos. R. Garza

———◆·▸◆◂·◆———

Camp No. 46

July 30 of 1862

5 miles from Rockport

Dear Sister,

We arrived here in good health some days ago. Three or four days ago I wrote my Mother but I don't know if she'll get my letter because one can't depend on this post, the letters have to go all the way to Shreveport, La. since there's no post between Washington and Tyler. Our regiment's health is poor. There are some 150 sick men here and we left some 175 others on the road. I assure you it's very sad to see them lying on the ground exposed to the sun and the air with the measles. But through good luck none have died. I've been exceedingly happy that Mr. [Bart] DeWitt and Manuel [Yturri] didn't come with us. If it's possible don't let them come over here because I suspect that from now on our perils will begin. Up to now everything has been very agreeable because you well know that for me everything is fine if I'm not pressured. The boys in our company seem to like me well. I'm in good health. I hear from you from time to time that you're enjoying the same health, and therefore I have nothing to complain about. In a letter, Elena wrote me that all of you had a lot of work because you got rid of the maid. I commiserate with you and for that good reason I don't expect you to write as often as you would if it were otherwise. Don't let my Mother live alone for you know she's up in years and something could happen to her and it would be a torment for us in the future, so take good care of her as she's the only one we have.[12]

Here where we're buried in the woods we don't know any news. There are endless rumors, but they don't have any basis and so I can't give you any news at all. I'm going to send this letter with a man who is going to Seguín. They discharged him because a horse left him incapacitated. This is what happened. Two or three weeks ago we were camped and we had just finished our day's work and consequently we fell exhausted. At night two brothers went to sleep on the floor (together). At about twelve at night some three horses tied close to the camp got spooked, broke their reins and took off violently in a rush and passed over these two poor brothers. One suffered some broken bones and we thought he would die, but through God's will he lived but he was incapacitated and it is he who is going home. The horse stepped on the other one's hand only.

Guard duty is being changed right now. It's very nice. All along the road when there were homes close by the ladies would come to see the changing of the guard. The guard consists of a leader for the day who is a captain, a lieutenant, a sergeant, two corporals and 24 soldiers. I'll be on guard duty tomorrow or the day after. My turn comes every eighteen days. It should be every thirty days but since there are lieutenants who are absent or ill, for those of us who are well our turn comes more frequently. There should be 30 lieutenants. Fannie Finney's husband is here, he's a lieutenant and a very good man.[13] One of his brothers is a soldier in his same company. Jos[eph A.] Costa is a 1st Sergeant.[14]

Eugenio and Pedro have enjoyed good health, they're very happy. The three of us live very comfortably in one tent. Pedro just finished his guard duty he's been on for 24 hours. The other three Mexicans are enjoying good health, Antonio Bustillos, Antonio Suniga and Simon Garza Placera.[15]

What a great desire I have to see all of you. You can't imagine what a great pleasure and joy it would be for me to return to San Antonio this moment, but there's not even any hope. God knows how long I'll be navigating these neighborhoods. I wish this would end so I could see Leonardo, for it's been such a long time since I've seen him that it seems to me that I don't even have a brother. But by just remembering him I desire to see him. What a great joy it will be for my mother to see her loving son, it would be enough to rejuvenate her and if God grants me life and health, I'll give her that joy before returning to San Antonio.

You'll give very many greetings to all our relatives, the Navarros, Cassiano, Na. Mariquita, Aunt Gertrudes, the Lockmars, Ed Rivas, the Leales, the Bug[i]nor[s], the Garcias, Ign. Cas[s]iano, the Rodrigues, Edmunds, Dwyer, Elliot, Cadenas, Daguerre, Yturri, DeWitt, and Josef M. Garza.[16]

Trueheart	Crawford	Carolina[17]
Margarita,[18]	Chepita[19]	3 boys
4 boys	4 boys	
Yturri	Jos R. Garza	
Elena	Eugenio Navarro	
1 boy	Pedro Ville Sarats	

and all the rest I may have forgotten.
Your brother who desires to see you,
Jos. R. Garza
To: Mrs. Bart J. DeWitt
San Antonio

Camp No 52, Near Pine Bluff
Jefferson County, Arkansas
Camp Holmes, 50 miles from Little
    Rock
August 20th 1862

Dear Ellen,

I take the opportunity of Lieutenant [Robert B.] Harvey going to San Antonio to send these few lines.[20] I suppose you recollect I promised you that I always would let mother know of my whereabouts. Until the present time I have nothing to complain of. I have enjoyed myself as well as can be expected under the present circumstances. This morning we had a shooting match for a rifle (6 shooter). Each company furnished a man, the best shot was to have it. Our company, represented by Antonio Suniga, came off second best. If Manuel had been here I have no doubt but he would have shot for it. It is such a long time since I received a letter from home that I do not know what has become of him. I hope that hereafter you will write if it is only three or four times every week or two to let me know the state of our family. You can not know how troubled I am sometimes. Awful dreams will visit me once in a while. By directing your letters to Little Rock I shall always receive them. [Eugenio] Navarro and Peter are getting along finely. In the course of time we will all be good soldiers. Every morning we have drill [and in the] evening battalion drill. I think it would make you laugh if you were to see me drilling my barefooted squad. We divide the company into several squads to drill. I take those that can not go out on the parade ground and teach them the manual of arms. Our camp at present is perfectly new having arrived only three days ago. The men are hard at work every day cleaning the grounds. This regiment is the best organized and better drilled and better armed than any which has come from Texas. Two or three miles from here there are four regiments encamped. One from Texas the others from this state, Ark., but none can compare with this. I am extremely glad that we joined it. It is true it takes us from home a considerable distance but we had to leave home one day or another so it does not make much of a difference after all. Lieutenant Harvey, who is a perfect gentleman, is going to San Antonio with the object of buying clothing for the men. If Mother can send me some good cloth, I wish she would (there is nothing to be had about this country). All she has to do is to make a good bundle, mark my name on it [and] place it in a box and hand it over to Lieut. Harvey. He will bring over anything that Navarro's family wants to send him. Also Cassiano and Peter['s], can be put in the same box.

I do not know how long we will stay at this camp. All the Yankees have left Arkansas, but I hear that they are coming to Texas by the way of El Paso.[21] I hope and pray they will never arrive at San Antonio. How I wish I was there now.

I wish mother would subscribe to the San Antonio *Herald* for me.[22] Anything that comes from San Antonio makes my heart glad. We hear sometimes of the great battles fought in Virginia and other places but you get the particulars as soon as we do and I do not see any use in referring to them. Whenever any battle is fought near us or we should happen to be engaged in it, I shall then let you know all the particulars. I suppose all my old friends, young ladies and young men, are either dead or gone for I have not heard from them since I left Eagle Lake. Erasmo Chaves I suppose came back from his trip and died or else why dont [sic] he write to me. Really I begin to think that as soon as a person is lost from sight he is lost from mind. Hereafter those persons who have forgotten me shall be drop[p]ed from the list of my acquaintances. If [James L.] Trueheart, [John C.] Crawford or Manuel happen to see one of these blue soldier-over-coat I wish he would buy it for me and send it for it will be awful cold in this part of the country. But cloth for coat and pants tell mother to try and send me some. Let it be one solid color. Military buttons for [the] coat [and] if you can find any [a] few strong drawers, two or three check shirts, etc. Really Elena, I would like to write sixteen pages to you but I can not find anything to interest you. The young ladies in this state, the few that I have seen, look miserable pale and thin. I have not seen a real beautiful girl yet. The men are not very patriotic. We arrested two, one for treason the other for depreciating the Confederate money. I have just been hearing some accounts of the Battle at Virginia, it must have been awful but the Yankees are pretty badly whip[p]ed.[23] They were whipped at Rich Mountain, Cumberland Gap, Baton Rouge and at Mis[s]ouri, so every where they had the worst.

I am getting to be mighty lazy. I can not pass the day without sleeping two or three hours after dinner but in the morning I have to get up at 5 o'clock in the morning. If Trueheart, Crawford, Manuel Cassiano or any of my friends are in town tell them to call on Lieut. Harvey and make his acquaintance. Any particulars you want to find out of this Regiment he will inform you. I would like to continue writing but have nothing more to say but to give my love to Mother, Rudecinda, Carmencita, Margarita, Chepita, Carolina, Elena, Antonio, [and] to all my nephews, nieces, relations, friends etc., also on the part of Eugenio and Peter. Send me some paper and envelopes. Tell Erasmo, Fermin, and Miguel Garcia to write to me. Misses Lockmars have not answered my letters, yet tell them I am waiting for an answer. Also Misses Margarita Navarro, tell them if they do not answer pretty soon I shall cut their acquaintance.[24] With my love again to Mother I remain your,

Brother, Jos. R. Garza

This will make the 7th or 8th letter I have written without receiving an answer.

———◆◆◆◆———

Arkansas Post
Oct. 2nd 1862

Dear Mother,

We'll leave for White River (Clarendon) in two or three hours. The Yankees are committing atrocities close to that place and our troops are going to concentrate to give them a good battle. To get to this point (Arkansas Post) we marched all day and all night because we got news that the Yankees were going to take this point. When we arrived, which must have been around three in the morning, our spies gave us the news that they had already crossed the river (they must have been about 2,500). We've already been here some 12 days.

Yesterday one of my friends received a San Antonio newspaper where I saw the news that Jose[ph M.] Dwyer had married Miss Anita.[25] I give him a thousand congratulations and I wish him happiness for in my opinion he hasn't done a better thing in all his life. Dear Mother, three long months have gone by without getting a single line from home. I've written letter after letter but no answers. Eugenio received a letter from his sister probably some two weeks ago where she said that all of you were well and it is the only news I've received in the three months from my home.

Eugenio and Pedro have been well, desirous of participating in some action. I don't write more often because of lack of paper, they gave me this piece. I don't know why I don't receive any letters unless the reason is because each post that comes once a week brings letters for the Captain and others without fail. If you write address your letters to Little Rock, Co. H, 6th Regiment, Texas Infantry.

Day before yesterday there was a general review of all the brigade. I didn't have the pleasure of seeing it because I was on guard duty. The review was held a mile from the camp. Navarro tells me that it was very nice. I figure that if we don't receive a little warm clothing we're going to freeze this winter, but God's will be done. And we'll see if we can take enough [clothes] from the Yankees to dress ourselves. Pedro is telling me right now that Fermin is surely dead because he hasn't lived up at all to his promise to write us. Tell Erasmo that I'm well and desirous of knowing about him, to write me once in a while. What has happened to [Bart J.] DeWitt, for I haven't heard a word?[26] It seems that all my relatives and friends have already forgotten me completely. Never in my life have I had such a desire to know about those at home until now. I read such bad news in the San Antonio papers about the scarcity, etc. that I'm desirous of knowing how you manage at home. Sometimes I imagine you don't even have anything to eat. For God's sake, write and let us know. I hope to God all of you are well. Don't worry about me (and tell them not [to worry about] Navarro and Pedro) in the least for we are men and we are fighting for our country. As soon as I can I'll let you know where and how we're doing. Give many greetings and remembrances from us to our families, relatives and friends.

Your son who desires to see you,
Jos. R. Garza

————◆◆◆◆◆————

Arkansas Post, Ark.
Dec. 9th 1862

Dear DeWitt,

Day before yesterday I received yours of the 23 Oct. & 5 Nov. I was sorry to learn you had been sick again, but glad at the same time. Glad, because it prevented you from comming [sic] to this outlandish country. You would have died long ago. Never think one moment [of] joining us. This is no fit place for you. Mr. [George H.] Sweet acted right in persuading you not to come.[27] Pneumonia broke out in our brigade about a month ago and we buried from three up to fifteen daily for two weeks. "What do you think of it?" You could not hear anything but the dead march from morning to night. We are putting up log cabins for winter quarters. Yesterday I was hard at work at our cabin, but today I do not work being officer of the guard. I was extremely sorry to hear of Llaguno's accident. I hope he is well ere this! When is he going to marry? If two or three hundred dollars will do you any good let me know. I'll manage some way to send them. I have no use for this article here.

I am glad to hear old Father [James] Giraudon is well, and still remembers me.[28] Next time you write to him remember me kindly to him. On the 22 of Oct. I wrote a long letter to Elena. Has she received it? Why don't she answer? To Carolina I wrote sometime before but I have not received a line from her. If they only knew how glad it does make me, I have no doubt but they would write oftener. My excuse for writing but seldom is the scarcity of paper. It is only when I receive a letter that I better myself to procure a sheet. We have been putting up trenches, rifle pits, etc., in expectation of the Yankees comming [*sic*] up as soon as the river rises. We took a Yankee prisoner the other day and he says that the abolitionists are comming [*sic*] in strong force as soon as their gunboats can go up the river about the 1st of Nov. I think we would have had a little skirmish with them. They came by land to about thirteen miles from here but could not come any further on account of the bad roads. They turned back to wait a better opportunity. General [Thomas James] Churchill is in command of this division.[29] Eight or nine regiments are camped about here. We expect to have enough time in a month or two. Never come to Arkansas, you would die of cold feet in two weeks. I never suffered of cold feet in my life until now. I tell you, you may roast them by the fire for three hours, turn around, step on the ground for a minute and they are cold again.

Dec 10th. I could not finish yesterday. I had to make my guard report, etc. Last night I had to sleep outside of a tent and this morning I found myself covered with one inch of frost. Today I have to go to work again at our shanty. We have it nearly finish[ed]; all that is wanting is dobbing and fixing the chimney. Yesterday a wagon load of things came for some of the men from Austin but nothing for me. I suppose my things will be along when the other wagons arrive from Shreveport. We expect them daily.

I hope you will get along at the Powder Factory.[30] It appears to me that it must be a very pretty business. If I can help in any way you know I am always willing. I hope Mother is well. Tell her not to be anxious about me. Navarro sends his love to his family and all of ours. He is well and [in] fine spirits. My love to Mother and the rest of the family. Trueheart, I suppose, is doing very well. Carmencita, what has become of her? Is Crawford running his mill yet?[31] How does he manage to buy wheat, etc.? I send you a fifty dollar bill to distribute amongst all my nephews and nieces for a Christmas present.

Tell Manuel to stay away as long as he can. He is not compelled to come. I would hope to see him here for the same reason that I would you. Neither of you come a step into Arkansas if you can help it. Your services will be required in Texas soon enough. I wish I was there. My regards to all inquiring friends. Your Bro.

Jos. R. Garza
(I am going to work.)

Austin Tex
April 17th 1863

Dear Mother,

Horatio Stephenson lent me sixty *pesos* ($60.00) which you will please do me the favor of returning as soon as you get this.[32] One can't travel now without it costing five or six pesos a day. Tomorrow I leave for Dallas, I couldn't stay in Victoria, it's very sad and ugly. McAllister told me he was going to San Antonio. I believe that by now he's there. He sent all the soldiers home. In a few days they will report where I'm going. There is nothing new. I went through Columbus and saw Vicente Martinez.[33] He told me Anto[nio] Garza, Anto[nio] Navarro and Carlos Sandoval were there but I couldn't see them.[34] They were most probably with their wagons or in Alleyton. [Tell] Elena not to fail to write me to Dallas. I wrote you, Mr. DeWitt, and the Navarros from Victoria. Elena shouldn't feel hurt because she already knows that writing to you is the same as if I wrote to her. This morning I went into a store and found music, but it was so old that I didn't want to buy any. I bought Isabel some little guitar pieces. If I find some pretty pieces for the piano I won't fail to send them to Elena and Carolina. Greetings to all. I almost got the courage to go to San Antonio but duty comes first and I couldn't stay more than a day. Well, it's better I not go and so make believe you saw me. Goodbye, your son,

Jos. R. Garza

Austin, Texas
May 15 of 1863

Dear Mother,

I've been well up to now. I haven't had any misfortune. The mules
I have are very untamed, but nonetheless we're doing well. I took a
hundred *pesos* from your pocket-book to pay for a chair I bought. It
cost me $80.00. Paper money here has the same value as in San An-
tonio, it's not worth anything. I leave this afternoon. Greetings to all.
Your son,

Jos. R. Garza

Shreveport, La
July 7th 1863

Dear Mother,

Tomorrow we leave, I think, for Na[t]chitoches. I don't know if
we'll go further than that or not, but we're headed that way. Always address your letters to this [place] until I write you again and tell you for
certain where I am. I hope you've enjoyed good health. I haven't heard a
single word as to how the family is. Nothing new except that now that
I came to the city I saw some thirteen federal flags captured by General
Taylor, very beautiful flags. Praying that you and the family are well, I
remain your affectionate son who desires to see you.

Jos. R. Garza
Lieut. Jos. R. Garza
17th Consolidated Regiment

Capt. Jno. J. McCown's Co.[35]
Shreveport, La.

———◆•◆◆•◆———

Camp Salubrity
Near Natchitoches, La.
July 31st 1863

Dear Bart,

I can't imagine the reason why my letters have not been answered. I have written to you several times and also to Elena. I hope to God nothing seriously [*sic*] has happened in our family. Do write to me dear Bart and let me know. I have not heard from home since I started. As far as concerns myself I have been as usual always in good health. The other day I saw the notice of the blowing up of the powder mill. I hope that it is repaired by this time and at work once more. Who were those men that got killed at the time?

On the road from Shreveport to this place we had pretty good times, only some days it was very hot and sultry hard marching but I went through with it very well. Once in a while [we] got some watermelons, also some very good water. Generally through these piney counties the water is excellent. The camp where we are now is watered by several springs. It is a very pretty place. It used to be a resort for the families of the adjacent towns in summer time. A part of General Taylor's army camped here when he was organizing for the Mexican War. Permits are granted to two men out of each company to visit the town of Natchitoches every day. I have taken the opportunity to go only once. I was very much pleased with the town. It must have been quite a lively place once upon a time, but now the river which used to run at the foot of it has changed its course and the shipments have to be done at Grand Ecore four miles from it.[36] I have not been at Grand Ecore but I am told it is a very small town on the banks of the river. I would not be surprised if one of these days the Yankees would pay it a visit. We have several guns mounted at the place. I don't know but we might have to make regular fortifications. There is some talk about it. If we do I am afraid it will turn out like my key at Arkansas Post, however, I hope not. Walker's Division has just arrived.[37] They are camped about three miles from here. McCulloch's Brigade is detached and ordered to join [Maj. Gen. Richard] Taylor.[38] It will leave in a day or two.

For about two weeks I have been in command of our company. The captain is away after some deserters. I get along very well. We have rank & file 60 odd men in a day or two when we will get some men belonging to our regiment now in Walker's Division we'll have over 70. I am first lieutenant of the company.

I had to leave my trunk at Shreveport. If any thing should happen to me send for it. I left it in charge of Mr. C. R. Harrison at the Four Miles Springs, Shreveport, La.[39] The heavy coat you made me a present of I left also. I did not wish to ruin it before I had use for it. I think this winter I'll have opportunity to send for my clothing.

The parson of our regiment is getting up a great religious revival. He has meetings nightly. Over two hundred men attend regularly. Yesterday he called for volunteers to build an arbor. Men turned out promptly & they built the best arbor I ever saw. Three hundred men can be easily accomodated inside. Next Sunday he said he would divide the men in *Bible* classes, i.e., in regimental and brigade.

Enclosed you will find a little ballad composed by one of the men of the brigade.[40]

Col. [William H.] Trader who was our brigade commander has been superceded by Gen. C[amille Armand] J[ules Marie, Prince de] Polignac.[41]

Give my love to all the family & friends. I remain as ever

Your Brother,
Jos. R. Garza
Direct your letters:
To: J. R. G.

> Company "16" 17th Cons. Regiment
> Gen. Polignac's Brigade
> Shreveport, La.

I spoke with a man from Vicksburg who told me he had seen H. B. Adams.[42] He was well.

I have written to Mother about ten times. Has she received any of my letters?

—————◆◆◆————

> Camp in the field
> Near Alexandria
> Sept. 9th 1863

Dear Bart,

Since I wrote to you from Camp Texas we have been marched up and down considerably but still have not met the enemy as yet. The report is that the Yankees are about fifty miles from Alexandria from 20 to 70,000 strong (which I do not believe; there might be about 15,000). Part of our division is close to the enemy. The picketts have met several times, no damage done.[43]

I am sorry to tell you that many of the men composing this division have gone home and I am afraid many more will go. No help for it. Yankees are close by and I suppose they are afraid. We have orders to be ready at a moments warning to start to wherever we may be wanted. I was in hopes of receiving a letter from you ere this, but I have been disappointed. Only once have I had the pleasure of hearing from you. I hope all at home are well. Write to me soon.

Tomorrow two men from our regiment leave for Texas to procure clothing for the men. I want nothing thank goodness. I even had to leave some of mine at Shreveport (don't forget, my trunk is at Mr. C. R. Harrison near Shreveport, La.).

I have just done my dinner composed of boiled beef and corn bread.

Do you get as much now a days? Many of our soldiers grumble at this poor fare, but for me I have not seen the thing that has made me dissatisfied yet. When I went into the service I determined that I would go through and I am of the same mind yet with the help of God.

With Jos. Costa I wrote to Mother and sent her $300.00.

Money is worth here as much as in San Antonio. It is a perfect shame the way they depreciate it. I see the articles in the newspapers appear not to make any impression on the minds of speculators.

Send me a San Antonio newspaper with social news.

Give my love to Mother and all the family.

Your Brother,

Jos. R. Garza

I am well, our regiment stands the highest at present in this division.

The other two regiments composing our brigade are nothing to brag on. Bad name, very low down. I expect you have heard of them. They are called Alexander's and Stevens.'[44]

Remember me to all friends.

JRG

Camp at Evergreen on Bayou Rouge, La.[45]

October 2nd 1863

Dear Elena,

Days, weeks and months have gone by and I have not even received a line from you. I am tired of writing home but it seems all of you have forgotten me completely. If it weren't for other persons who have written me I wouldn't know that all of you were well. How much work can it be for you to sit down and write a few lines? You have everything necessary, so what is the reason for your not writing me? Even DeWitt who used to be so punctual in answering my letters now is the same as you and all in my family. You don't have the excuse of saying that you don't know where I am. I expect that from here on out you will not fail to at least let me know that you've received my letters and that all are well. Enough of complaints.

Since the last letter I wrote you we've moved to different camps always with the objective of being closer to the enemy. But up to now we haven't had any encounter. We thought we were going to have one in a short time but now it seems that the Yankees have retreated. We are camped close to the Atchafalaya River. This area is worth defending, you would enjoy seeing these very wealthy plantations and the very magnificent homes. But the gardens are what have caught my eye. How beautiful they are, the trees so well formed. Here you'll see some in the form of an armchair, over there some as little living rooms with doors and windows with tables and benches inside. The cedars are so tall and perfectly arranged. The walkways have flowers everywhere. I assure you it is extremely beautiful. I wish you would see them, you'd desire to possess some like them. No where else have I seen things taken care of with such meticulousness as in this area. It would be sad if the Damn Yankees were to take possession. There are innumerable cane fields. I've never eaten so much cane in my life. Eating a cane is a gift when marching half suffocated from the dust. It is so beautiful to see so many soldiers marching two by two on the road. Our line with equipment and everything is about five or six miles long. Our brigade is now by itself, for security, the others went by a different road. I think they will see the Yankees; no telling when we will.

I'd like to know what Manuel is doing and where he is. I already desire to see all of you again. I hope to God my Mother is well. Why don't you write me and tell me everything that's going on. Fermin wrote me the other day but he doesn't say much. The only one who has answered my letters has been Miss M. Brown for which I am grateful.[46] Through her I'm informed of the health of all of you. If you're curious to know what I wrote her tell her to show them [the letters] to you, I think she'll do it.

Fermin told me that D[o]n Policario and B and A had taken a trip to Monterey. I hope they enjoyed themselves. How are Vicenta and Edmunds? I haven't heard a word from them. Edmunds promised to send me some newspapers from time to time but he hasn't done it. I'd write some more but I don't have anything to say. I'm in good health. A thousand greetings to all.

> Your Brother,
> Jos. R. Garza
> Address your letters to Shreveport.

October 3rd. Tomorrow at 4 we leave for [the] Atachafalaya River. 400 Yankee prisoners passed through here today. They're being taken to Alexandria.

———●◦●◦●———

> Camp 3 miles from Washington, La.
> Oct. 16th 1863

Dear Bart,

We are expecting to meet the enemy in a day or two, maybe sooner; we are fifteen miles from them. Green's Brigade has been fighting their advance guard.[47] All our men are in good spirits.

The number of the enemy I can not inform you. Some say they are 10,000 some more and some less. My opinion is that they are pretty strong or else we would have attacked them ere this. We have a goodly number of troops around here. I am sure we will give [the] Yankees a rather tough tussle.

We carry nothing with us but cooking utensils and a blanket each that we pack on our shoulders (i.e. blanket). The nights are getting pretty cold but we make very comfortable beds out of moss and we make out to keep warm two or three of us bunking together.

Yesterday I saw Capt. Harrison and his brother.[48] He is looking the same as ever. He asked me about you. He is now about a mile from here, Green's Convalescent Camp and train.

The other day I wrote to Elena. I hope she received my letter. I have not heard from home for a long time. I wish you would write to me.

1/2 doz are waiting for this pen and I have to hurry. It is getting dark too. My love to Mother and all the family. God bless them all. I am well.

Your Bro.

Jos. R. Garza

Remember me to my friends. Our Brigade has been exchanged from Walker's Division to Morton's. I don't know how we will like it yet. We were very well satisfied with Walker.

———◆◆☀◆◆———

Camp on Bayou Boeuf

Near Cheneyville, La.

Oct. 27th 1863

Dear Mother,

We're already back and we haven't had any encounter with the enemy. The pickets are the ones who have fought them every day last week. We were close enough to hear the rifle shots. Now we are retreating. The Yankees are pursuing us. I don't know where we'll stop.

I'll tell you a little about the life of a soldier.

The 12th of this month they ordered us to march forward taking with us only a blanket and cooking utensils. Everything else they sent back. That night it rained cats and dogs, all of us, of course, like ducks in the water. We marched about 30 or 40 miles and stopped 15 miles from the enemy. Several days we heard the roar of the cannon and we waited for orders to engage the enemy but instead they ordered us to retreat. We fell back about 15 miles with the Yankees advancing on us. Every day our cavalry and theirs fought, killing one or two or three and injuring an equal number.

Last Saturday our regiment and another one went on picket duty 10 miles back. We had just gathered enough firewood, grass and straw for beds, etc. when [we heard the shout] get up boys, the Yankees are coming. We took battle positions. Our major who was in command of our battalion went to see how far the Yankees were. He returned running and shouting, load they're upon us and in fact we began to hear the shooting getting closer (they were about 500 Yankee cavalry who were coming fighting with our mounted troops). We were in line formation about half an hour and seeing that the Yankees were not coming we retreated 1/2 a mile within the brush (we had orders not to light fires and it was a very cold day). The Yankees retreated and we returned to the old camp. We again lit our fires, cooked corn bread and meat from our backpacks and ate dinner. Then we went to bed about 7 in the evening. We slept well until 9 at night when they awoke us and sent our company of pickets with orders not to return until three in the morning. We left and marched about 1/2 mile and stopped. The captain then sent me with sixteen men a 1/2 mile further according to his orders. That night we didn't sleep. How cold it was. (How I've missed my clothes I left in Shreveport.) At three in the morning we returned [and] at that time everybody was awakened and we retreated three miles. We were there for several hours. At about twelve noon we left, retreating, marching all day and all Monday. Today, Tuesday, it may be that we rest. The Yankees are advancing little by little. They say they're some forty thousand. Today, or, more correctly, last night, we caught up with our wagons with our clothes and for the first time in two weeks we changed into clean clothes. This life is good for me. I'm in good health, always happy except when the mail comes in and there are letters for everyone except me. Since I left home I've received only one letter from all of you and that was the one that Mrs. DeWitt wrote. I haven't heard from anyone since September.

I've written regularly. I wrote DeWitt on the 16th of this month and Elena a little before that, etc. I'm desirous of hearing from all of you. Write me. Greetings to all.

Your son,

Jos. R. Garza

PS It may be we might not stop until we get to Shreveport.

All the plantations are destroyed. Some appear not to have been inhabited for years. It is sad to see everything ruined. Now that the Yankees are coming they'll finish desolating everything.

Don't worry about me. If you hear that they killed or wounded [me,] tell them that it's okay, he died well. May God help him, he didn't go to eat candies when he left to defend us, I prefer to hear that he died fighting rather than his being buried in the kitchen.

Goodbye. May God preserve you.

Your son,

J. R. G.

———◆◆◆◆◆———

Camp at Harrisonburg, La.

February 20th 1864

Dear Elena,

I received your esteemed letter of January 11 on the 11th of this month. I hadn't answered, not because of a lack of desire but because the day I received it I had just finished writing Mr. DeWitt and not having anything else to say, I let time go by until today.

In Mr. DeWitt's letter I told him about the encounter we had with the enemy and so I don't think I need to repeat that. I'll only tell you that if you had seen our retreat from Vidalia you would've burst out laughing. Imagine a regiment of soldiers marching, behind these fifty or sixty mounted on mules (untamed, one-eyed, and maimed which our regiment took from the Yankee cavalry). The mules had ten or a dozen blankets as saddles, a little rope or chain as a bit and the rider was shouting, laughing and beating the mules. Here you see one stumbling in a hurry over there another rolling down from his mule with blankets and all, others bucking and the soldiers yelling. I assure you that it's more beautiful seeing it than writing about it. I mounted a big mule. It had about twenty-five blankets for a saddle.

The man who was wounded in our company is recuperating. He's in Natchez. The other two we lost I believe must also be there. I hope these two and some others who left our regiment don't take up arms against us because if we ever catch them, God help them.

When we crossed the Tensas River in retreat several of our company jumped into the water because the boat was sinking but by the grace of God there were no mishaps.[49] We got here in good condition and spirits the 9th of this month.

Day before yesterday I wrote Eugenio Navarro and Pedro again. They haven't yet answered any of my letters. I also wrote Leonardo but I believe he hasn't received my letter.

I'm very sorry to learn about the death of Guadalupe's wife and also about the illness of . . . daughter. I hope [the illness] doesn't disfigure them. Give the whole family a thousand expressions [of sympathy] on my part.[50]

Major [W. A.] Ryan of our regiment leaves for Austin day after tomorrow and I'm sending this letter with him.[51] Tell my Mother not to worry about me, that I'm very glad and happy and that I'm not as lazy today as I used to be. Two of my friends and I built a very beautiful and comfortable little house. We worked hard for a day and a half. We built it from pine logs and the roof of lumber, eight feet long, six feet wide, and seven feet high. We covered the cracks with straw. The furniture inside consists of a bed for the three which takes up half of the house, a little table in one corner and my trunk in the other, guns and sabres hanging all around. I assure you many are envious but they're so lazy that they don't want to build one for fear that we'll have to move in two or three days and they don't want to leave their work behind. But we three don't care, we always try to build something comfortable if we have time. Here I am today, very comfortable writing, using my trunk as a chair. It's very cold and there's sleet, but I don't even care, I'm very comfortable in my little home.

Many of our officers have left and they're going to their homes on furlough. But I don't want to request one until the month of September or around there unless there's some need. But thanks to God my presence is not necessary at home. My Mother doesn't need for me to take care of her, instead she takes care of me, therefore I'll stay where I'm needed.

Fort Beauregard has been reconstructed.[52] I believe we'll stay here for some time. I like this place very much. The Ouachita River doesn't have enough water. The gun boats can't yet come.

I've just gone to see Major Ryan. He tells me he might not leave on Monday but he is going over there anyway. Tell Mr. DeWitt that I'm sending Capt. McAllister $330.00 and the overcoat with Maj. Ryan. Tell him I couldn't sell the overcoat, they wouldn't give me what I asked for it and so I thought it was best to send it. I have the knapsack here in good condition. When I go there I'll take it.

February 21st

I'm also sending a letter to Capt. McAllister with the major, but nevertheless tell Mr. DeWitt to go see him and tell him.

Tell Margarita [Isidra] and M[aría] A[ntonia Romalda] Navarro that I'm not writing them now because I don't have anything new [to tell them] but the next letter I write over there will be addressed to them.[53] This is the way I write, first a letter to Mr. DeWitt, after a week or a little more I write you, a little more time goes by and I write to Margarita or M. Antonia. I write my Mother more often than to all of you.

Don't think I don't desire to hear from all of you, for I assure you that nothing would give me greater pleasure than receiving a letter every week. I have no doubt that if you took a little initiative you could very well write me three or four lines giving me news about my Mother's health and of all the family. I don't want more, just write me this and I'll be satisfied. Use pencil or ink, it makes no difference. Tell Captain Trueheart to expect a letter from me one of these days. Tell the boys that I haven't forgotten anyone, that when I return I'll give them all their Christmas gift. My most esteemed remembrances to all my family and friends, especially my Mother.

A brother who loves you,
Jos. R. Garza
Write to:
Co H, 17th Consolidated Regiment
Polignac's Brigade
Shreveport, La.

———————

On Picket near Harrisonberg, La.
February 26th 1864

Dear Mother,

Having the opportunity of sending these few lines to San Antonio with the son of Mr. Wooback [Wurzbach] (the irrigation ditch commissioner), I write you to tell you again not to worry about me.[54] I'm well, enjoying good health, desirous that you take care of yourself and live many years. I wrote Elena four or five days ago. I sent the letter with a lieutenant from our regiment. I had thought of sending it with the major but he hasn't left yet. Everything is quiet around here, there are no Yankees.

Your son who desires to see you,
Jos. R. Garza
Greetings to all.

The man is waiting, I don't write more.

Your son
From
J .R. G.
Mrs. Josefa M. Garza
Care of Jno. C. Crawford
San Antonio, Texas

———————•❖••❖•———————

Near Minden, La.
Hdqrs Waul's Brigade
Walker's Division in the Field
Apl. 19th 1864

Friend Bart,

Having a few leisure moments, I thought I could not better employ them than by writing to you. Our command having been halted at this place to give the men an opportunity to wash and clean up generally as they have been marching and fighting for the past month without rest.

I have some painful news to communicate to you. It is that Joe Garza fell while gallantly fighting at the head of his company at [the] Battle of Mansfield on the evening of the 8th inst. He was shot above the knee with a shell and died soon after. This I was told by a number of his company who had assisted at his burial. Joe spent the greater part of the day with me the day before the fight and was in fine health and spirits. I saw Manuel yesterday. He was looking very well and he requested me [to] inform you of Joe's death.

I have had a pretty rough and hard time since I reached this command as it was falling back from Marksville where we were going and the Yanks pursuing. As I had to relieve the then quartermaster of this brigade and everything being in confusion, I had a pretty rough time. I did not get into the battle of the 8th but did in the 9th. It was a hard fight but we whipped the Yanks badly. I think it was the most complete vic-

5. Buried on the field at Mansfield, Joseph de la Garza's remains were later returned to San Antonio by his brother-in-law Bartholomew DeWitt and interred in San Fernando Cemetery No. 1. Photograph by Jerry Thompson.

tory of the war. We had but about 8 or 9,000 men in the first day's fight and in the second about 12,000. The enemy had not less than 30,000 in the first and were reinforced on the 2nd [day] by a fresh corps. They were completely routed losing about 300 wagons & trains, wagons loaded with stores, between 80 & 100 ambulances, 16 pieces of artillery with everything complete. All these fell into our hands, and were saved. They also destroyed [quartermaster] stores without number. Small arms it would be hard to estimate the number as all of our gun supplies [and] Enfield rifles [that were left] on [the] battlefield and there were wagon loads hauled off. As far as I was able to see and could learn from the parties sent out to bury the dead, theirs was at about 5 to 1 [to our dead]. And hundreds are reported lying in the woods, the men not taking the trouble to bury when there were none of our men killed. In prisoners we got between 4 & 5,000. Our loss in officers has been terribly severe. We have to mourn the loss of Maj. Gen. Tom Green, Brig. Gen. [Jean

Jacques Alfred Alexander] Mouton, some 9 or 10 colonels and others in the same proportion.[55]

After the 2 days fights we were ordered on this march. Where we [are] going is "Quien Sabe" but am inclined to think Arkansas is the point unless [Maj. Gen. Frederick] Steele should happen to fall back to[o] rapidly that then would be a chance for us to catch him.[56] Whenever we may go I will be content as long as I enjoy my present good health. I have met again many of my old friends since I have been out here. At the head of them Pow[hatten B.] Bell one of the best soldiers in this Army, but now [the] poor fellow is sick in the hospital at Shreveport.[57] I have made it known to some of our mutual friends so that he will not want for anything. I am very much in hopes that I will get him with me.

I am compelled to close this rather abruptly on account of a pressure of business.

Please remember me kindly [to] Miss [Alice] Sweet & Mrs. A. & Miss Annie.[58] Also to your wife and all inquiring friends. Hoping to hear from you,

I remain your friend
H. B. Adams[59]

Part 2
Letters of Capt. Manuel Yturri

"Military life is the most miserable there is in this world."

—MANUEL YTURRI,
MAY 7, 1865

6. Serving until the breakup of the Trans-Mississippi Confederacy, Manuel Yturri rose to the rank of captain and returned home to San Antonio, where he became a prominent rancher and public figure. He died on February 26, 1913, at the age of seventy-five. Courtesy of John and Helen Yturri.

Camp Gillespie
May 31st 1862

My dear wife:

We arrived at Fredericksburg yesterday morning about 5 o'clock. Martial law was read to the inhabitants by Capt. J[ames] Duff and afterwards by Mr. [Fritz] Messinger in the German language, our company stood before him while he was reading it.[1] After the law had been read in both languages, Captain Duff ordered thirteen men to be placed on the different roads, streets and lanes, and not to let any person pass without having a pass from the provost marshal.

About half past ten o'clock A.M. my turn came around, and I had to guard until 7 o'clock P.M. We did not get to the camp until half past seven or eight o'clock, and you cannot form an idea how I felt. I never had been tired as much in my life as I was this time.

We are at present camped at about a mile from the town.

I am indeed very well pleased with the company, and all the men seem to be very kind and accommodating, all well behaved.

I am indeed under great obligations to Captain Duff and Lt. J[ames] R[obert] Sweet for having me detailed on duty in their company, and hope I will never get out of it until the war is over, or die in it by their side, for I think that Captain Duff and Lieutenant Sweet have proved to be very kindly towards me and this favor I will never forget as long as I live.[2]

I am in the same mess where Y. Cassiano, José García, and Severo Losoya are, and all seem to be very well satisfied and pleased with the company.[3]

Write to me soon and tell me all the news, and direct your letters— Fredericksburg—

Private M. Yturri, Capt.
Duff's Co., T. P. D.[4]

The rest of my friends can not write for they have no paper to write to their families at present but will buy some tomorrow, while writing this José Garcia came in with some letter paper from town. I had to borrow this sheet of paper to write you these few lines.

I am very well, but feel a little tired from the march, but will get over it in a few days.

Remember me kindly to your Mother, Carolina, Vicenta and to all who may inquire about me.

Yours,
Manuel Yturri

———◆•✦•◆———

Brownsville, April 9, 1863

My Dear Wife:

You can't imagine the feelings I have and which I've felt for several days since I got here. The reason is that two days after Lieutenant Colonel Duff got here I ran across him and we greeted each other, etc., and he asked me where I was and I told him that I was with Col. [Philip Nolan] Luckett's Assistant's Office.[5] He then told me he was very happy that I was in that position and today he again told me that since Capt. [Richard] Taylor had not taken me with the rest of the company which left for the mouth of the river, he sent an order on Friday morning for me to report to the camp.[6] The camp is four *leguas* from here[,] where Lieutenant Colonel Duff's battalion is.[7] But Taylor and the company are at the mouth of the river and seeing that[,] the colonel told me that it was better for me to leave for the camp[. A]fter having told me that he was very happy to have seen me at the office, I went and spoke with Gen. [Hamilton Prioleau] Bee and I told him that I suffered from hemorrhoids and that it hurt me a lot to ride on horseback and I also told him about my experience with Duff.[8] What he is, is nothing but a hypocrite. I'm going to do everything possible to move to Capt. Pedro Cevallos's company in Colonel Luckett's 3rd Regiment, or to have them send me to my company whose members I think are going to get together in Victoria this month.[9]

In camp they make them exercise three hours every day. Duff sent the order and Lieutenant [Samuel G.] Newton and several of the company told me so that I would leave but General Bee has not yet signed it.[10]

If you had an inkling of what I feel in finding myself in my present situation, I don't know what to do. I feel like I've been in the army for years, and I can't tell you what I'd give to be by your side. I'm almost crazy. This is only because we see that we don't know when this war will be over and if I'll have the pleasure of seeing you again, which is what I most fear in this world. Why don't you write me more often? You worry me greatly. Since I left San Antonio I've only received two letters from you. I'm tired of writing Edmunds and asking him to send me money. I'm suffering here without a penny.

I'm sending you the money you requested in Captain [Dominick] Li[ve]ly's wagons with other things he's sending Señora French.[11] The package is addressed to you care of Venice y Hermanos, but I don't think it will get there before 15 or 20 days.

Write me soon and tell me all the news. Write me a long letter and tell Vincenta to write me and also Jesus.

> Your loving husband who desires
> more to see you than write,
> Manuel Yturri
> Mrs. Ellen Yturri
> San Antonio, Texas

———◆◈◆———

Camp Slaughter[12] Feb 14th 1864

My dear Elenita:

Yesterday I received your esteemed letter dated the 3rd of this month in which you tell me that it's very strange for only your letters to get lost. Well it isn't my darling because many are lost because there are two regiments of the Third Infantry, but the other one is of the state and sometimes due to error they send the letter to the other regiment and that's how they get lost since both are of infantry. There are many persons in the regiment who have also not gotten their letters. Well, my dear, it's sometime now that I'm receiving your letters very frequently for which I'm very happy and I hope that I'll always receive them. You tell me that you sent the ring to be fitted and I hope it fits you well and you take care of it. They say that coral is very good for sickness of the eyes and that one never has any eye sickness if you have it on. I believe it's better not to wash it much with soap and water because it loses its luster. The way I gave it luster was with a little primer and rubbing it with wool. As to the things I sent you, Lieutenant [Julius] Hafner has already received a letter from his wife that she had received the first package.[13]

I'm amazed that you sold the corn and shucks so soon.[14] Why didn't you wait a little? If you can, sell everything for silver. Paper isn't worth anything. In Houston they say that they're paying twenty-five and thirty [dollars] for one [bushel of corn]. Whenever you sell the shucks and corn ask for a good price and in silver if possible. How much silver do you have? It's good to guard everything you have well and spend only what's necessary. You tell me you bought provisions from the government for the first time. What did you buy? You were foolish not to have bought before because I wrote you more than two months ago that you could buy what you needed from the government and when Edmunds was with me in Houston, he promised me that he'd get you everything you needed from the government, but I see it was your fault and his that you waited two or three months without obtaining provisions. Today it's one week that I sent you the order and a certificate form in case you had to present one. I knew perfectly well that it wasn't necessary for you to present one. You tell me that you were unable to find my order of corn and shucks which Edmunds has. Well, it's not exactly an order but it's the number of bushels and the bunches of shucks which belong to me. It's written in the booklet if I'm not mistaken. Look for it carefully again.

You tell me as always that Lito is neither better nor worse from his illness.[15] Well, this is what saddens me most, that he doesn't improve at all. But you always let it go, when it may be too late and he can't be

7. The oldest son of Manuel Yturri and Elena de la Garza Yturri, Manuel Yturri III
was only eight months old when the well-known German-born artist Carl G. von
Iwonski painted this image of him in San Antonio at the beginning of the war. Later
in life Manuel, or Lito as he was known in the family, became deputy district clerk for
Bexar County, the third generation of Yturris to serve in public office. Born on January 19, 1861, he died on June 26, 1933, and was buried in Mission Burial Park No. 1.
Oil on canvas, 12 in. x 10 in.; the painting is signed, "Sept 19th 1861/C. G. Iwonski
frt." Institute of Texan Cultures, UTSA, 073-1147. Courtesy of Helen Yturri.

8.   Carl G. von Iwonski was one of the better-known antebellum painters and photographers in the Lone Star State. On the eve of the Civil War, he painted Manuel Yturri in a hunting costume with his favorite hunting dog, Guess, and a brace of ducks. The work, in a private collection, is the only known full-length oil portrait by the artist. Von Iwonski is shown in this 1866 image in his San Antonio studio. An oil portrait of Joseph de la Garza, painted posthumously, possibly from a photograph, can be seen in the background. 072-0751, courtesy of the Institute of Texan Cultures.

cured. You'll probably remember when there's no available remedy. Poor soul, it may be that this illness takes him to the grave. If possible don't give him meat and coffee to taste, it is better for him. Does he know how to dress himself or do you have to dress him as always? They tell me that he's very chatty and very fat and also that he calls you stinking dog, tricky pig, etc., when you make him angry. I believe this is all the result of your spanking him too much and you make him angry and he's fearful of you. I've always told you it's very bad to strike a very young child and of his temperament, you already know that he has the same temperament as Vicenta, and I ask you to please not hit him until he has the understanding of a five or six year old. And who's taught him these words? Don't let him play with any neighbor boys who can teach him these bad customs. Teach him to read and count, rather than to say such ugly things and not know how to count and not say the alphabet yet. Don't let him be out in the sun. Take good care of him as I have great sympathy for him because of his sickness. I fear he'll never be well, don't hit him, talk to him with love at least because he remembers his dear father so much. Who does our daughter look like, you or me? And Vicenta's, who does she look like, her or him?[16] You tell me that old lady Rymand is in the city with Chepita and that when you were there you left your best shawl that you had on the bed and it disappeared.[17] I'm surprised that you left it on the bed knowing what she is. Don't ever invite her to see you because you'll have nothing left. Her son still in this regiment is well.[18] My friend [Henry] McCormack sends you many remembrances as always.[19]

Day before yesterday I wrote you and sent you a ring of coral in it for you to deliver to Vicenta. Tell her it's very difficult to obtain the beads on the ocean shore.[20] Here everyone knows me only as Yturri and since I enlisted with that name without putting Castillo that is why I address you E. Y.

Tomorrow morning we leave for [the San] Bernard River to relieve the guard.[21]

Many kisses for Lito and our daughter and all those who remember me.[22]

Have you received the cloth I sent you or not? When you go to town go see Mrs. Hafner to see if she received Mr. Hafner's; his and mine went together.[23]

> Yours until death,
> Manuel
> Mr. M de Yturri Castillo
> Care of Mr. E. B. Edmunds, San
> Antonio

———————◆◆◆◆◆———————

> Bryan's Plantation, February 24th of
> 1864

Dear Elenita:

Yesterday afternoon I received your very esteemed letter dated the 14th of this month in which you tell me that you had not answered before because the children have been sick of fever and colds and you also tell me that our daughter is already talking and that her hair is very long and very curly about which I'm very happy and it's better, my dear, that you never cut it. I'm also very happy to know that Lito and our daughter love each other very much and that they miss each other when they're apart. You also tell me that you wish I were there to see them. My darling, who wouldn't want that joy more than I?

My dear, you tell me that you're going to charge old man Crail 25 silver pesos for the house and 15 to Solya and Mr. [A.] Eule and five to the painter; well, you do what you think is best according to what rents are now.[24] Ask DeWitt or Edmunds, because if they don't pay you in silver, how can you pay silver for what you buy? Sell the corn and shucks for silver. You tell me that from here on out you're going to collect the rent; I'm very happy and I believe you'll be able to collect the rents better than I and at the same time you can learn much. When you can't make out a receipt, ask DeWitt or Edmunds. Don't fail to take care of the little money you have and also buy everything you need from the commissary, provisions, etc., every first day of the month. Don't waste time, my darling, and buy everything you can, candles, sugar, flour, etc.

Yesterday Lieutenant J. Hafner received a letter from his wife in which she tells him that she has already received everything. It would, therefore, be good for you to go to her house and get the cloth I sent you, [and] needles and thread. I don't have the time to write you a long letter. This time, I'm officer of the day today and I'm very busy. Have you received the ring I sent you for Vicenta in a letter?

Many kisses for Lito and our daughter and you receive many more from your old man. Say hello to Y. and Edmunds and give his daughter a kiss.

Say hello to all who remember me.

Yesterday I received a letter from Mr. J. [De]Witt in which he says that he's a sales clerk in the cotton office and that they don't know what they're going to do with the company but I've been so busy that I haven't answered his letter.

Take good care of Lito and our daughter. Lito doesn't know yet how to dress? Teach him to count and read.

Yours until death,
Manuel Yturri
From Lt. M. Yturri, 3rd Tex. Inf.
Mrs. Manuel Yturri
San Antonio, Texas

———————◆◆⋇◆◆———————

Nava Sota [Navasota][25] March 20th
of 1864

My dear Elenita:

Yesterday afternoon I received your very esteemed letter dated the 1st of this month and at the same time I received another one from

Captain [John R.] Rosenheimer dated the 14th of the present month in which he tells me that you went to see him the same day he got there and that he had given you the buttons and money I sent you.[26] You don't tell me if you've received the rings I've sent you and the other things. You tell me you're thinking of moving in May to the house where Mrs. Binns lived.[27] Well, do what you think is best, but to me it seems you're going to be very sad if you're going to live by yourself.

Why don't you ask Tata to go sleep at night at the house you're moving to?[28] Tell him I asked you to ask him, and if you want, I'll write him. In case you have to hire a servant, it's better that Tata lives at home with you if you think it right and he wants to do it.

My darling, as to the note that Tata has, pay it. It's money he lent me when I was in San Antonio. The day I left he gave me two hundred pesos and before that he had lent me [more]. Pay him whatever I owe, the note bears my signature. It's true I told him that he could rent the house for seventy pesos, but now you can tell him that you have to rent it for more if you think so because you can't live from the rents [alone]. Write Tata a little note and pay him what I owe if you can and ask him how much of the rent from the lot he has rented to Major [Simeon] Hart is mine.[29]

The first call for drills is already sounding and I don't have any more time and to make things worse the pen is very bad and also the ink. Excuse the poor penmanship.

When I was in Houston, I went to see Mr. Theo[dore E.] Giraud and he told me about the death of his wife.[30] How is Lito of his illness? Many kisses to Lito and our daughter.

I think we'll leave for Louisiana in 3 or 4 days.

> Your faithful husband,
> Manuel Yturri
> Write me:
> Lieut. Manuel Yturri
> Comdg Co. F, (Lucketts) 3rd Regt.,
> Tex Vol. Infty

Care of Capt. C. C. Clute, Express
Agent[31]
Houston,
Texas

Many greetings to all those who remember me. Write me often, my darling.

Yours until death,
M. Y.

———◆•✽•◆———

Camp near Douglas[32]
April 6th, 1864

Dear Wife:

It's been more than two weeks since I've received a letter from you, so that I don't know if you've received the things I sent you. I believe that if you wrote me they sent the letters to Shreveport. As of today we've traveled for ten days since we left Nava Sota and I believe that in seven or eight days we'll get to Shreveport. At times we travel twelve, fifteen, eighteen and twenty miles a day and on foot so that when one gets to camp one arrives very tired.

Sunday I saw Doctor [George] Cupples in Crockett and last night he camped close to our camp and he and I and Lt. J. Hafner conversed until after twelve midnight.[33] Talking to him in Crockett, I asked him what was good for Lito and he told me that it's not good to operate [on] him, that it's foolish, that he's taken care of many who had that illness and that he's cured them in two or three months. Don't allow any doctor to operate [on] him. He says that after an operation it's good to always wash out the intestine before putting it back in and after washing it to rub cooking oil with a cloth and push it inward so that it doesn't become so swollen. My darling, take good care of the poor boy as I believe he must suffer greatly.

I sent you a letter with Lieutenant Payne of Nova Sota [*sic*].[34] Did you get the letter, did you receive the letter and photograph I sent you from Houston with Mr. Campbell and did he go to visit you or not?[35] My dear, when you write me I want you to tell me if you've received my letters and from where and what date so I can know if you have received all the ones I've written you.

How is Tata? Is he in San Antonio? If you see him ask him if he took out the carbine I left at the home of Jacobo Linn, the gunsmith.[36] And tell him to take good care of my two-barrel rifle.

When you write me tell me what Mr. DeWitt is doing. [Did] Ygnacio Cassiano join the army or is he with his family? And what does my *compadre* Fermin do?

I don't have time for more, I'm on guard duty and they're calling me. Many kisses to Lito and Leontíne and you receive many more from your husband.[37] Take good care of my clothing, don't let it get moth eaten, put it out in the sunlight once or twice a week. I told Mrs. T. Giraud to send you my trunk as soon as she had the first opportunity and when you receive it take everything out and put them out in the sun, don't let them get holes, they might get moths. Many greetings to all who remember me.

If you see Capt. Jno. Rosenheimer, tell him that 3 from the company deserted, Meliton Hernandez, Marcos Garza and Andres Gonzales and Eduardo Postel of Company D.[38]

My darling, don't fail to get all you can from the government each month, such as sugar, flour, cloth, etc.

Write me as always. Where is Jesus?

> Your loving husband who desires to
> see you more than write,
> Manuel Yturri
> Mrs. Manuel Yturri
> San Antonio, Texas

Camp near Alexandria, La.

May 22nd, 1864

My Dear Elenita:

I'm very happy to write you this short note and inform you that I'm in good health. And I hope that you and our two little angels are also enjoying the same. We arrived here some two or three hours ago. We're camped some three miles from Alexandria, but the Yankees almost burned the whole city during their retreat down the Colorado [*sic*; Red] River.[39] I don't know how long we'll be here.

My darling, how is Lito and his illness? How is your mother, Carolina, Chepita, and my *comadre* Margarita? I believe my *comadre* [and] your mother must have felt the death of my *compadre* Jesus exceedingly. I felt it tremendously and cried very much since I considered him my best friend in this world and the friend I most appreciated since I came back from college and since he and I had very frequently talked about becoming partners and setting up a store after the war if God permitted us to see the end. You've still not moved to our house? If you do move don't forget to tell Tata to live in the little room. I've already written him and I told him to live in the room so that you won't be sad or alone. I don't want you to be alone in the house and get sick of something in the middle of the night or something happen to you or some drunkard come by. Only God knows what might happen to you. Treat Tata well and talk to him. You know he's very serious; if you need him to do something for you ask him. How much flour, sugar, candles, soap, etc., do you get from the government each month? How much does it cost you to live each month? Doesn't Mr. DeWitt take out firewood from the quartermaster each month? Tell him to ask if you can take out [goods] and if you can, I'll send you a requisition. When you write me tell me if you received my trunk and the clothes in it and take them out so they won't be moth-eaten and also the pair you have stored so it won't be damaged. For right now if El Tiburón comes soon send me two pairs of shorts and two of socks and my jacket which is in my trunk.

Many remembrances to all our relatives and all those persons who ask about me.

Many kisses to Lito and Leontine and you receive the most from your affectionate husband who desires to see you more than write you.

> Manuel
> Address: Lt. Manuel Yturri
> 3rd Texas Vol. Infty
> Waterhouse's Brigade
> Walker's Division
> Marshal, Texas

How is San Antonio now, doing well or poorly? What is Ignacio Cassiano doing and my *compadre* Fermin? And what is Tata doing now? Since we left Texas we've traveled at least four days at a time before resting and at best we've rested after two or three. For more than two months we've rested two or three days at a time and we take off; our feet are already like the hoof of a horse. The marches we undertake are for eighteen to twenty and twenty-two miles per day and occasionally 14 to 15, but only very rarely. Only an iron constitution can endure this kind of life; the roads are so dusty and there are so many of us that when you get to camp we can't recognize anyone because of the dust and our legs and feet are like those of Negroes, and our meals consist of ham and corn bread, every day the same thing. What a life! You can believe it only if you see it. I think that if I survive this war you won't catch me in another one in this world. What a good lesson! I wouldn't miss it for a million if I come out okay and in good health.

> Yours until death
> Manuel

Camp in the Field, La.
June 18th 1864

My Dear Elenita:

I'm going to write you a long letter as I promised in my last one, and tell you all the details of the battle we had close to the Saline River in the state of Arkansas. Our forces arrived at Camden, Ark. in the afternoon and the Yankees had left the day before. By the time the sun came up all the enemy troops had crossed the Washita [*sic;* Ouachita] River and so they had almost a forty-eight hour advantage on us and we went out the following day in the morning with two day's ration which each of us took in his knapsack and one blanket. We couldn't leave during the night because our wagons did not arrive until very late that night and we had to cook and eat dinner and prepare ourselves so that we could follow the enemy in the morning. We left all our transport behind, wagons, etc., and we did not see them again until two or three days after the battle.

Camden is a very beautiful city and almost as big as San Antonio and the Yankees had it very well fortified and it is at a high elevation and we couldn't attack it without having lost many people.[40] The general's plan was not to allow them to receive provisions and see if that way they would surrender. But the Yankee general smelled that our troops had them surrounded and during the night they started to cross the river. They burned more than two hundred wagons and they threw some artillery pieces into the river and they retreated as fast as they could in the direction of Little Rock, Arkansas. We pursued them for two days and all along the road they were throwing and burning such things as clothes, feather and cotton mattresses, wagons they had broken and many other things.

The third day we left around three in the morning without having eaten anything or having anything to eat; we had finished all the rations we had brought. And as soon as we left, it started to rain and rain[ed] until about six or seven in the morning almost without stopping. About eight in the morning we started to hear the shooting. By then we were about a mile from the enemy and our cavalry was fighting the Yankees.

By this time we had traveled some sixteen or eighteen miles and the mud was up to our knees and in some places we had to cross creeks where the water came up to our waist and in some parts above that, and the woods were full of many pines. The Yankees had already expelled part of General Price's cavalry and infantry and some Negro Yankees had taken some artillery pieces. General Walker moved us about in a hurry for about an hour, moving here and there until he found out where the enemy was and we formed a battle line.

We had just finished forming ourselves properly when the enemy which was concealed behind fallen pines began to shoot. We couldn't see anything except their heads and chests and the dancing of the soldiers on both sides began. The shooting lasted about two hours and a half or three without stopping. The Yankee forces were about nine or ten thousand and our division about five or six thousand. About half an hour before the battle ended General [William Read "Dirty Neck Bill"] Scurry came to order us to fix bayonets, and having just given the order and fallen wounded, and all the rest of the soldiers having no more than four or five cartridges, we did not fix bayonets, and other soldiers did not have cartridges and this was the principal reason why we did not fix bayonets.[41] But if General Scurry had not fallen wounded we would've fixed bayonets and taken most of the Yankees prisoners because upon the last discharge we shot at them they left and our cavalry did not pursue them and so they took very few prisoners. The battle occurred about a mile and a half from the Saline River. They call it the battle of Jenkin's Ferry.[42] If we had not been so tired we would've pursued the Yankees. They left the armament that the Negroes had taken from our troops.

I assure you my darling that it is very sorrowful to see the wounded, some with a shattered arm, some with a leg, others with head wounds, others in the spine, legs, hands, etc. Six in my company resulted wounded, but one of them mortally, dying five days after the battle. His head was injured and we could see his brains. He fell close to me; he was a little behind me and he fell in the water and I raised him, but seeing the bullets which were flying every where, I told him to lie down because there was not even a pine close by to protect us and it was best for him to lie down.

In the end he died crazed. General Scurry fell wounded close to me and he died the following day. General [Horace] Randal was also wounded but he died two days afterwards.[43] We lost two generals from our division and General [Thomas Neville] Waul was wounded in one arm.[44]

In the afternoon they went to bring the wounded and I was still missing one of my men in my company. And the following day I went in the morning with twenty men to bury our men and to look for the missing man but they had already taken him to another hospital and so I couldn't find him. After we got to our battle camp I told the soldiers to begin to gather the dead from our regiment. My intention was to continue to look for the wounded individual I was missing while burying the dead. It had rained so much that it was mostly water and mud and we didn't have shovels with which to bury the dead. I then went to the Yankee hospital to borrow some shovels but they told me that they didn't even have anything to bury their dead. I then returned to our battle camp and I told the soldiers to make shovels from wood and they began to dig a big grave to bury everyone together. We buried six soldiers, one corporal, and one lieutenant, all from our regiment, on a mound and the grave was only a foot and half deep because if we dug deeper water would gush out. [T]here were dead from both parties but more Yankees. Most of the Yankees were wounded in the head and chest. In parts both Yankees and our own were found dead together. There were many dead Negroes and some fourteen wounded. One Confederate soldier went to the hospital and killed five or six of the Negroes who were wounded because the Negroes had decapitated his brother after he was wounded in a battle.

It is an ugly thing to see a camp after a battle, to see the number of dead people and the blood. We lost some eight hundred dead and wounded and the Yankees some one thousand eight hundred. After the Yankees had retreated we found one hundred eighty dead they had thrown in a creek close to the battlefield.[45] They burned all their wagons and they threw some artillery pieces in the Saline River and they took their wounded in mules to Little Rock. If our troops had not been so tired they would've captured almost all the Yankee army. We captured some two hundred wounded more or less. The day of the battle and the following day we had nothing to eat except some corn on the cob which we toasted and a small piece of ham they gave us.

※

Camp in the Field
La., July 3, 1864

My dear Elenita:

It's more than a month since I've received a letter from you and I write you by every mail service. I don't know why it is, you either don't write me or the letters were lost. Henceforth, I want you to write me more often and tell me all the news and if my *compadre* [Otto] Amilong [Amelung] paid you the eighty *pesos* in paper money I lent him and if he took my trunk from the home of Mrs. T. Giraud in Houston.[46]

I found out there was a very great flood in San Antonio. Write me and tell me all the particulars.[47] Have you moved to the city and are you living in our home? Did Edmunds or Vicenta ever come visit you? It's been some four days since I've been a little sick but I'm well now. The first day I had a fever and I vomited a lot and had a very severe stomachache from the colic but I think it's from how well we live, on lean meat and corn bread. Many times [we eat] meat and coffee made from corn without sugar. What a sad life I experience as a soldier, my darling. Almost all the soldiers in the division suffer from diahrrea [*sic*]. Meat and corn bread are the rations.

How is my little son Lito? Has he gotten well from his illness? And has our little daughter started to talk? And how are you? Fat and beautiful I think because at least you live better than I do. I'd love to eat your leftovers, my dear; I think I'd be very happy. From here on out send my letters to the following address

Lt. M. Y., 3rd, Lucketts,
Regt. Tex. Vol. Infty

Care of Capt. C. C. Clute, Express
    Agent
Houston, Tex
This way:
Lt. M. Yturri, 3rd-Luckett's Regt.,
    Tex Vol. Infty
Waterhouse's Brigade, Walker's
    Division
Care of Capt. C. C. Clute, Express
    Agent
Houston, Tex.

My darling, write me very often since I'm very sad because I don't know how you and our two little children are. The only pleasure I have is receiving a letter from you.

Greetings to all those who remember me.

Yours until death,
Manuel

———◆◆◆◆◆———

Camp in the Field, La.
July 23rd 1864

My Dear Elenita:

We are at this moment preparing to leave and make camp some 40 or 50 miles from here on the Black River or Trinity River, I believe in one of the two.[48] My dear, this letter will be delivered by Don José María Belasquez who a few days ago, along with Don. Teodoro Zepeda of our company, obtained their discharge and at this moment are leaving for San Antonio.[49] Don Belasquez has been our cook for a long time and if he stops at our home, I want you to treat him as well as you can. If you need him hire him, he's a very good man and very honest. I've never seen another person take such good care of things as he. Take him to my grandmother's house and yours when you go with the children. I recommend him highly and hire him if you need him and if mother wants to hire him for some things like whitewashing homes, etc. If by chance you need him don't hesitate to hire him, he will help you greatly. He does not know anyone in San Antonio so let him sleep in the kitchen or wherever you think best. He's bound to help you greatly for errands and in the kitchen, etc. Hire him full time if you like him, his ways, etc.

Many remembrances to my mother, my grandmother, my *comadre* Margarita, Chepita, Carolina and all my relatives and all those who remember me.[50] And you and our two little children receive great love from your affectionate husband who desires more to see you than to write to you,

Manuel

Write me more often.

Sra. Doña Elenita Yturri

By Conduct of Don José María

Belasquez

San Antonio, Texas

. . . And that night we slept on the wet ground and covered ourselves with one blanket which was all I and Lieutenant Hafner had. Lieutenant Hafner had left his pillows with General Scurry at the battlefield.

My darling, I'm now becoming very thin because the only thing we have to eat is lean meat and beans once in a while. Our coffee is a cup of water. Our breakfast this morning was a cup of water, a few beans and a little ham in the beans and corn bread without lard. I want to be a private in Texas [rather] than an officer here. One can at least eat better and see one's family every four or six months. My dear, I have a great desire to go see you and our two little angels but it's impossible to get leave, at least for an officer. I'm tempted to resign and be a private, maybe then I could go see you after what seems years of not seeing you. A soldier has greater opportunity than an officer to go back home. My dear, when you answer this letter tell me if Tata showed the letter to Robert Franklin or if he took the liberty of opening and reading it.[51] If that is the case I want to know so I can write him a letter and if God grants me life and I return to San Antonio I'll inflict some good slaps by which he'll remember me as long as he lives so that he never again opens someone else's mail and shows it around. The scoundrel will have to pay for that. Woe to him if he took the liberty of opening my letter and showing it; that will cost him some good slaps on the face, as the Spaniards say.

My dear, during the battle I wasn't frightened at all and I wasn't afraid either. I was just waiting to fall dead each minute. I had already prepared myself in case I had been killed and I didn't think of anyone except God and you and our two little angels. But what hurt me the most was that I [would] be killed and you would marry again and my two little children be treated badly and that you would forget to give them a fine and complete education, this is what I felt the most, that you would marry and forget about me and our two little children. But may God not permit that you ever think of doing that if it were my turn to die.

I was amazed that wounded fell on every side of me and I didn't receive even a scratch. Some who were in front of me and others behind me and on the side fell wounded, but it wasn't my turn to die. It is truly pitiful to see the hospitals after the battle, with piles of arms, legs, and hands, it seems like a slaughter house. What an ugly thing. When I returned from burying the dead, I stopped to see one of my soldiers who was in the hospital, and of the twenty men I had, one of them upon seeing the legs and blood, fell and fainted and others could not see the legs being cut off nor see them afterwards. I have seen very much since I became a soldier and I can't tell you everything nor the hardships I have endured, etc. I would rather be a shepherd than a soldier in the front lines. A young, very handsome officer from our brigade who had the largest, most disciplined company in our regiment and who wore a black feather in his hat was quickly demoted to private because he acted cowardly and didn't advance but retreated behind his company. Now he carries a rifle instead of his saber into battle because of his cowardice.

My darling, don't forget to write me each week or more often, tell me all the news. Has Edmunds [or] Vicenta come to see you? Have you moved to our home? Did you lose anything in the move or did you break anything?

My love, there is no hope for now in obtaining a leave to go see you. Many greetings to those who remember me.

After the battle our soldiers found many pictures of the dead Yankees, of their families, fiancées, etc. I don't ask for yours because we might fight with the Yankees and I might be killed and they would keep your picture. I don't want that. When we first engaged in battle our troops made a very ugly retreat and I was afraid that the Yankees were going to make us flee but fortunately we regrouped and we made them flee, and they fled like quail.

Many kisses for Lito and Leontine. How is L's illness?

Write me very frequently.

> Yours until death
> Manuel
> Write me at
> Lt. M. Y., 3rd Tex Vol. Infty.
> Waterhouse's Brigade, Walker's
> Division
> Marshal, Texas

P.S.

Day before yesterday I spent almost all day washing eight changes and a pair of gloves, and the following day in mending them. Soap can't be found, it's very scarce here. I had to go about nine miles to obtain a little. Everything here is very scarce, provisions, etc. If you can buy me some flannel and make me two over shirts and send them to me. Three pair socks, two pair drawers and send me the new pair of shoes that I left in my trunk at Houston if you have received the trunk. This is if you know any reliable person coming to the regiment.

Give my love to all inquiring friends.

> Yours until death
> Manuel

Mrs. Manuel Yturri
San Antonio, Tex.

———◆•◆◆•◆———

Camp on Bird Creek, La.
August 10th of 1864

Dear Elenita:

With great pleasure I write you these lines to inform you that I find myself in good health for which I have to give God thanks. Yesterday afternoon I received a letter from Edmunds of Houston in which he very bitterly complains because I haven't written him or Vicenta, and he says that I write to many in San Antonio except to him and V. and that he feels greatly offended being that they are the closest relatives I have, etc. But this is not true because I've written the two of them [and] if they haven't received the letters that's not my·fault. He also tells me in his letter that he's going to send me some handkerchiefs, socks and cigarettes, probably with Amilong.

He also tells me Vicenta & Elena did not agree; did you ever saw [*sic*] two women that agree; no! Neither [have] I. He tells me you were at Mr. DeWitt's home and that you, Lito and Timmy were well.[52]

My darling I expect you to treat them very well if they come to see you. If you see Capt. Lively or Lieutenant Phil P. Shard[e]in and they can bring me a pair of pants send them with one of them even if you don't send me anything else but a sturdy pair of pants for the outdoors not of fine cloth, and the jacket which is in the trunk; don't send me shoes.[53]

Day before yesterday I spent the day with a friend of mine in General Polignac's Division and I went to see Jesus's captain and the rest of my friends; all the officials and soldiers who knew him loved him greatly. The captain gave orders to hand me my trunk, saber, etc. The trunk is very far from here but if we go close to where it is, I'll try to get it and send it to San Antonio. I believe that by this time you may have weaned our baby girl. Take good care of Lito and our baby girl and you take greater care.

How is my dog Guess, dead or alive?[54]

My friend MacCormack sends you many greetings. Rosenheimer and Hafner are well.

Many greetings to those who remember me.

Where are you living now? Tell Mr. DeWitt to throw Mr. Eule out of the house and . . . don't rent someone else's house.

> Your affectionate husband who desires
> more to see you than to write you,
> Manuel
> Send me the latest news.

I don't have time for more, they are sounding the call for drills.

———◆◆━◆━◆———

> Camp near Harrisonburg, La.
> August 17th of 1864

Dear Elenita:

I've just received your letter and the things you sent me with Mr. [Martiniano] Rodríguez.[55] The poor soul has just arrived. I don't believe he'll be punished. I'll do everything possible so they will not punish him. Tell Mr. DeWitt to collect the money for the corn and shucks from Edmunds. The wagon belongs to Tata. If Mr. DeWitt does not collect the money for the corn and shucks from Edmonds, you yourself collect it.

My darling, I think that Vicenta has not said all of that about you, and if she has said it forgive her; God knows how to punish her. Don't believe, beautiful, everything they tell you. I'm as enraged that they talk about you as if they stabbed my heart. But I ask you to please forgive her this time. It may be that I won't ever get to see you and my two little angels or her again, and if I die I don't want you to live fighting like cats and dogs but that you treat each other as sisters. My dear, I ask you to forgive her as a last favor for me, for God will punish her.

I don't have time to write you more because the mail is about to leave.

Yours until death,
Manuel
Mrs. Yturri

————————•⬦••⬦•————————

Camp near Camden, Arkansas
October 8th of 1864

My dear Elenita:

At this time I write you these lines and inform you that I'm enjoying good health and I hope you and our two little children are also well. Captain Rosenheimer is going to stay in Camden until he receives an answer regarding his resignation and then he'll leave for San Antonio. We'll leave day after tomorrow for Washington, Arkansas, from what I hear and from there I don't know where to. We're now in such a situation that we don't know where we'll be going. One day we go to one place the next to another. Today I bought a pair of pants and I had to pay one hundred fifty-six *pesos* and two *reales* for them [so you] can imagine how scarce things are. I can barely live on my salary, I spend all of it on tobacco and clothing alone. I'm sending eight rings and two little ones for Lito and Leontine with Captain Rosenheimer. Oh, my darling, you can't imagine what I would give to be by your side, I don't think of anything else all day and during the night except you and our children. Occasionally I dream that I'm at your side and I'm playing with the children, and when I wake I find myself very sad when I find I'm in bed by myself.

I'm going to do everything possible to see if I can resign as an officer and become a private in Texas. I don't care at all to be a captain and I don't want to be one, what I want is to see you and our two little angels from time to time, even if I were a private. You can't imagine the work many of us go through here; many soldiers don't have shoes or clothing and also many of the officers are very short of clothing and shoes. Write me soon and tell me how many rings you received. I'm sending you two small rings and a large one in this letter, which are a total of eleven. Address your letters as follows:

> Lt. Manuel Yturri,
> 3rd, Lucketts Regt., Tex Vol. Infy
> Waterhouses Brigade, Forneys
> Division
> Shreveport, Louisiana

Martiniano Rodríguez sends you many greetings and he remembers Lito frequently; he thinks that there is no more beautiful and bright boy than Lito and Lieutenant McCormack also sends greetings.

> Yours until death,
> Manuel

Write me very frequently since it's been more than a month that I've received a letter from you.

Talk to mother about the debt I owe and tell me what she says; see if she wants to pay it and we'll pay her the interest; this is if she's willing and has the money.

> Manuel

Greetings to mother and all the family, my grandmother and family and all my friends who ask for me.

Write me more frequently, my love, you can't imagine the joy I experience knowing how you and our little children are. Only God knows if I'll ever get to see you. Who knows if I'll die here from some illness because this country is very unhealthy or the Yankees will kill me.

Have Edmunds or Vicenta ever talked to you?

Camp near Camden, Arkansas
October 17th of 1864

My dear Elenita:

Day before yesterday, Saturday the 15th of this month, in the afternoon I received your very lovely letter dated 29 September. We've just returned from some exercises. They executed a captain of General Waul's brigade and our division for having advised the soldiers in his company not to cross the Mississippi River when we thought we were going to cross it.[56] And he also told them that he was not going to cross the river and that he would join with them in Texas in a certain wooded hillock and that he would not blame them if they didn't cross the river. And I think more than twelve thousand of us men, I want to say soldiers, were present when he was executed.

I assure you it is a very sad thing to see them be executed. First they were brought in a wagon and on it was a coffin and the person who was to be executed and a minister by his side and a very sad dirge playing. Then they would unload the coffin and then the minister would pray and he and the soldier knelt. Afterwards the captain sat on the coffin and the guard unit comes to the area where they're going to shoot, twelve men from ten feet away and the leader of the guard unit gives the order to shoot, all at one time, and of the twelve rifles only six are loaded so that they don't know who kills them. The first of this month they executed a soldier for desertion but he cried before he was executed when the minister was praying with him and he knelt when they executed him although generally they're executed standing up. I assure you it's a very sad thing to see an execution. This captain they executed was forty-six or seven years old and he was very brave, he didn't even change color when he was executed. Besides the infantry guard they added two cavalry companies, one on each side, as guards. He was a married man and has family. Poor wife and family! How they will suffer when they find out.

My dear you can't imagine the joy I had upon receiving your letter and knowing that you and our two little children are well and that Lito is beginning to speak English and also that Timmy already understands everything. Do you now have the piano where you're living or is it still in Carolina's house? I want you to teach Lito English and to count and read and also Spanish in particular. Don't let him waste time, teach him how to read and count a little every day.

Our troops are digging trenches and building fortifications around this city of Camden. Apparently they expect an enemy attack here.

Captain Rosenheimer's resignation has been accepted and I think he will soon leave for [Texas]. He's in the city half a mile away and I can't go see him because I'm on brigade guard duty, but tomorrow I'll try to go see him. I'll send you eleven rings so that you can distribute them among my relatives as you see fit so that they'll remember me. It took fifteen days to receive this letter, it came very quickly. Write me more often and tell me all the news. I don't write any more because I can't see and my hands are very cold. Write me as always at Shreveport, La.

Many remembrances to all my relatives and friends.

Yours until death,
Manuel

I received an answer to the letter I wrote Edmunds where he tells me that Vicenta hasn't said even a single word about you and that he's surprised that you and I believe it. I wrote him a very strong letter.

Camp near Camden, Ark.
Oct. 26th 1864

My dear little wife:

I received your kind letter yesterday evening with date of the 3rd of October and one from Lt. [Enrique "Henry" Belleau] D'Hamel with the same date in which you wish me to tell you how I am and how I get along.[57] Well darling I have not been well for the last ten or twelve days. I have been suffering from the diarrhea and am not well yet and have not taken any medicines because I am a very bad hand to take them but will have to if I do not get better soon. Well dear the only thing that troubles me is that I can not see you and our two little children, I do not thin[k] about anything else. It seems that I have not seen you for years and there is no prospect of getting a leave of absence and God only knows when I will come home. I will be willing to sacrifice anything to be by your side. There is nothing that would make me more happy than to be at home. I have a notion to resign and be a private in some company in Texas rather than be an officer here and be so far away from you. If I knew I could join or they would permit me to join some command in Texas I would resign in a moment just to get to see you and our two little children.

Well dear, I am very glad to hear that the house you live in is very warm and am sorry that you have to pay so much for wood. Well dear, do not send me any clothes unless you send them by some responsible person. I am satisfied if I send you a requisition for wood it is nine chances out of ten that you will not get it for if the quartermaster does not wish to let you have it you will have to stay without it. I will send you a blank and speak to Gen. [sic] D'Hamel to try and get it for you from the quartermaster, although I have not drawn any wood for a year. I will send you a blank for the next month. Well darling, I see you tell me if I want you to be economical I must help you, have I not help[ed] you as much as any person can[?] You have not sent me a cent for over a year since I left home, Friday, Oct. 23rd 1863, nor do I wish you to send me any money while you and the children need it. Fifteen dollars that I borrowed in gold from Edmunds, while in Houston I had in my pocket for several months and never spent a cent of it and then I paid a hundred dollars in paper for five in gold, and sent you the twenty dollars by Capt. Rosenheimer because I thought you & the children would need it more than me. I do not want you to be stingy but at the same time I do not want you to be extravagant.

Dear, I do not think there is a man more economical than I am since I have been married and under the present circumstances I can not help you any, for the ninety dollars that I get in paper money, just pays for my washing and for the tobacco that I use. Write to me and tell me how much you get paid for the house Mr. Crail had and the one the Painter had and what your expenses are every month.[58] Paper [money] is selling here twenty-five and thirty for one in silver so that my salary comes to three *pesos* per month. My darling, how do you want me to help you when I am so far from you and I barely have enough to buy tobacco and to pay for washing my clothes and once in a while to buy a little package of wheat flour and sugar when I have money and they are available? With paper money you can't buy anything unless you give twenty-five to thirty *pesos* for one of silver and then you can buy sugar or flour. What do you think, my dear, we who have to live with only corn bread without lard and scrawny meat? I'm sick now and what I eat is lean meat cooked in water and corn bread without lard. How can I not be tired of being a soldier? Just think for a while and you'll see the troubles one goes through in this country. I'm tired of this bloody war and it seems that there will not be peace for one or two more years.

Tell Mrs. Hafner that her husband stayed in Harrisonburg, La. on the 25th of August and that about two weeks ago, I found out through a soldier who came from the hospital where he is and who came to see me that he was well except that he was very weak and that he was trying to obtain a leave to see his family.

Teach Lito and our daughter to read and count and speak English.

My friend McCormack and Martiriano Rodríguez send many remembrances.

Greetings to all my relatives and friends who remember me.

> Yours until death,
> Manuel

P.S. At this moment Lieutenant Hafner has just arrived and he's very fat and in very good health and he says that he's going to write his wife this afternoon.

I can not send you a requisition for wood today. I am very busy. I have to go to drill. I will send it sometime next month. The mail is going to close in a few minutes.

Manuel

Camp near Camden, Ark
Nov 13th, 1864

My dear Elenita:

I'm going to send this letter with my friend R[ichard] C. Daly, first lieutenant of a company of this regiment, who will leave tomorrow for San Antonio.[59] He's a perfect gentleman and I wish you to treat him very graciously if he hands you this letter personally. He's been sick with fevers and chills a long time and he's going to Texas on sick leave and see if he can recover his health. He's one of the most military of the officers we have and he gave me lessons on tactics for some time. Don't fail to invite him to visit you. If Mr. Crawford or my *compadre* Trueheart are in San Antonio introduce him to them and tell them to invite him to go to the ranch to spend a few days. Maybe he'll recover his health. He leaves in the morning but who knows if he becomes sick on the road, he's very thin and very weak. I hope his trip will turn out well.

My darling, write me very often and tell me how you are and how Lito and Leontine are and if Lito already knows the alphabet and if he speaks clearly and if Leontine has already begun to talk.

I believe Lieutenant Hafner will obtain a leave to go to San Antonio this month and when he returns I'm going to try to obtain one for myself. If I go, I'll take my friend Henry McCormack and he'll stay with us at home; so prepare a room and a bed for him. Don't forget my darling. The only thing is that the trip from here to San Antonio costs about a thousand pesos and I don't know how to get the money. If I had a horse and saddle it wouldn't cost me even one-fourth the amount. My dear, you can't imagine the joy I'd have if I could see you and our two little angels. I'd prefer to be a private and where I could see you than be an officer here. It seems like years since I've seen you, and I don't think of anything else. I'm even getting gray-haired from thinking so much about all of you and not being able to go see you. What I wouldn't give to be an eagle and fly to where you are. I think I'd go every evening and return at day break.

My friend McCormack and Martiniano Rodríguez send you many remembrances.

I can't write any more because my candle is almost gone.

Our division leaves for Spring Hill, Ark., at 8 o'clock in the morning because provisions here are very scarce.[60]

> Yours until death,
> Manuel Yturri

> At 8 at night:

You've never told me if you received the rings I sent with Captain Lively which Jesus had when he died.

Always mail your letters to Shreveport, Louisiana.

> Mrs. Manuel Yturri
> San Antonio, Texas

> Camp near Shreveport, La.
> Feb. 28th, 1865

My Dear Elenita:

In the last letter I wrote you I told you that we were going to leave the following day for Natchitoches, but the following day there was a counter order. I believe that tomorrow or the next day we're going to leave in the direction of Natchitoches. My dear, I don't know why it is that I don't get any letters from you frequently, for I write you almost every time there's mail service. What's the matter, my darling, that you don't write me? Are you mad at me or sad? I myself don't know how I feel at times, I stay two or three days in my tent without going out all day long. I'm very sad because so much bad luck has befallen on me in not being able to go see you as I thought.

Kiss Lito and our daughter and you receive the most from your faithful husband,

M. Yturri

I've been lying down most of the day because I have a pain in my legs or bones. I believe it's due to the soakings and being in the water so much and sleeping with wet clothes, etc. I believe that if I were single and I knew that this war was going to last four years more, I would kill myself. From that you can imagine if I'm not sick of this sad life. But my dear my time is taken up only in thinking about you and our two little angels. What a joy it would be if I could [see] you and Lito and our daughter who [must be] very grown-up. I don't think there's another more beautiful and bright boy in all the world. I don't tire of seeing his photograph and I also believe that there can't be another girl as beautiful as my little daughter. Take good care of them my darling and treat them well, don't spank them, beautiful, do me that favor and you particularly take good care and enjoy yourself as much as possible.

Many greetings to all my relatives.

> Yours until death,
> Manuel Yturri
> Send this letter to Venceslado
> Ximenes.[61]

Shreveport, La.
March 18 of 1865

Dear Elenita:

I have just gotten back from Natchitoches, La. I went to bring Jesus's watch and a ring and a pocket book. The watch is made of silver and is not working. The trunk and the clothes are in Keachi, La.[62] I left orders to sell the trunk and the clothes because most of the clothes are soiled and moth eaten and I had nothing to send in the trunk to Texas, and since there is much danger that the Yankees come to this part of the state they advised me that it would be better to sell them. I told the doctor who has the trunk and the clothes to sell them and send me the money. The Negroes stole many things. The only thing I found of value is a bag and a pair of gloves.

I went to visit my cousin Mary Picque in Natchitoches and she received me like a brother, or to express it better, like a mother.[63] She treated me very well and she looks very much like the cousin of the Rodríguez's. She has a daughter named Anita, very lovely. Never in my life had any family treated me as well as Mrs. Picque and her daughter. She and her daughter are by themselves. Her son, Carlos Vital Picque, is in Virginia. He's a lawyer. Right now he's wounded in Virginia. The division already left for Texas and I'm going to leave in half an hour.

Kisses to Lito and Timmy and you receive more.

Yours until death,
M. Y.

Greetings to all my relatives. It's already some two months that I haven't received a letter from you.

M. Y.

Piedmont Springs, Texas[64]
April 11th of 1865

Dear Elenita:

Late day before yesterday I got to this point and it was about half an hour ago that we received orders to leave tomorrow morning for Hem[p]-stead, Texas, where I think we're supposed to stay for some time.[65] My blankets have been wet for some five or six days because I haven't been able to dry them due to the bad weather we've had. It's been raining almost all the time, light sprinkles but enough not to allow us to dry our clothes over the fire. And tell me, my darling, if sleeping with wet clothes and blankets over a period of time doesn't bring about illness? I think that if I get to be forty years old I'll suffer much from rheumatism and it could be even before I'm thirty years old. Yes, my dear, this war has ruined all my physical well being for the rest of my life. It's been more than a week since my feet have been dry any one day. My shoes are torn and I have no socks, etc.

Write me soon and let me know all the news about San Antonio. How are Lito and our daughter? Teach them to speak English, to read and write and count. Don't let them waste their time or spend their time with bad company and learn bad customs. I want them to be well raised and for people to say how well raised those children are!

Many greetings to all my relatives, [and] friends who ask for me and you receive the most from your

Very Loving husband,
Manuel
Address your letters to Houston,
Texas

Take good care of my dog Guess. Does he still have the same collar I put on him? And if it fits him tight take it off and put on another one.

Manuel

Don't let the children spoil [the dog]. I hope he doesn't forget what I taught him.

When you answer this letter tell me all the news about weddings which have occurred recently and all the particulars.

> Yours until death,
> Manuel Yturri

———●◆◆◆●———

Camp near Hempstead, Tex.
April 26th of 1865

Dear Elenita:

I have just received your letter dated the 13th of this month in which I see that some of your letters have been lost according to what you tell me that you have written me several times. I have received only one where you tell me that Tata is in San Antonio.

My darling, here in our regiment everyone is very poor, no one has money. I owe eight *pesos* in silver which I spent, three for a pair of shoes, four for a used hat I bought, and one *peso* I spent today when I sent [someone] to buy coffee in Hempstead because I'm desirous of drinking it.

My dear, I've asked General Smith to release old Hafner as officer of muster rolls and then when I get an answer I'll ask for permission to go see you, but I doubt it very much that I'll get it because we have only four service officers in the regiment. But if they don't give it to me I'll resign and since I only have twenty men in my company I don't have a right to have another officer. But I think that by next month I'll be able to tell you definitely if there is any hope of going to see you.

Well, my darling, what alarmed me the most upon reading your letter was to see that you tell me that Lito is better although he's limping. Well, what happened to him? I haven't received any letter in which you tell me that he was injured. Take good care of Lito, my dear, don't let him and also our daughter out on the street or with bad company.

Well my darling I will do everything possible to try to get a leave for next month. My dear, apparently you think that I don't try to obtain a leave, but you're very wrong. There's an order that no company can be without an officer present and this is what keeps me. If old man Hafner had been a gentleman and hadn't deserted, I would already be by your side without a doubt. But under the circumstances my friend McCormack can't do anything for me. Regarding the money I told you to send me with Capt. Daly or with A. Ryman, I wrote you from Camp Magruder in Louisiana and I also wrote you not to send me the money with Hafner because I was afraid he would not return, but it looks like you didn't receive any of my letters.[66]

It's raining and I can't write anymore. Kiss Lito and our daughter and you receive many more from your loving husband. Tell me how Lito hurt himself.

Many greetings to my relatives and persons who ask for me.

Yours until death,
Manuel Yturri

McCormack and Capt. Daly and M. Rodríguez send you remembrances.

Write soon and address my letters to
Houston, Tex.

I think we'll soon move to Liberty, Texas.[67]

<hr />

Camp near Anderson, Texas[68]
May 7th of 1865

Dear Elenita:

Some days ago I received a letter dated 12th of February and I hadn't answered it before because we're traveling and we reached the camp very late and we left at sunrise. In it you tell me you already moved with Mama and that you rented the house for fifty *pesos*. I wish you had been able to rent it for eighty *pesos* [but] I'm very happy that they paid you ahead of time.

You tell me that Lito has become very spoiled. I don't like that, my darling. It is best to stop that right away because if you don't do it now, much less later. It won't hurt him.

I'm very happy that Lito and our daughter are very big and speak much English and Spanish. I'm happy that Tata is in San Antonio and that Lito loves him greatly and I expect that our daughter will also love him greatly and I want them to call him Grandfather. I'm glad that he visits you often, and don't fail to treat him well and tell him to come frequently and teach the children to respect him as a grandfather. Tell him to write me. I've already written him several letters and I haven't gotten an answer from him. Is he old and very thin, or has he not changed at all?

Last night I received one of your letters from San Antonio dated 17th of last month in which you tell me that Mr. Hafner had left for here and that you were very sad because you hadn't sent me the money with him. Well I'm very happy that you didn't send me the money because he left for Mexico from what I've heard from persons who have received letters from San Antonio and if you had given him the money, I would never have gotten a cent of it, and besides, I had already written you several letters where I tell you not to send me anything with him, but I believe you haven't received them. And I also told you in one of them to send the money if not with Major Newton then with Lieutenant Daly who is now captain. He got his promotion yesterday and more reliable persons than these you can't find and you won't have a better opportunity. But I think that my letters must not have reached you. However, you can send me the hat, socks and two colored shirts and overshirts with collar with Binceslado Ximenes.[69] Tell B. Ximenes that I've already received the doctor's certificate. Tell him that it's been some time now that I've been reporting him absent due to illness in the hospital. He's in no danger now but tell him to come as soon as possible.

Tomorrow we'll get to Piedmont Springs close to Millican where we were camped last year.[70] And I think we should stay camped there for sometime. So don't forget to write very often and give me all the news. And I want you to send me the eighty silver *pesos* as soon as possible because I need the money very much. But don't send it unless it's with a very reliable person.

I saw in your letter of the past 17th that you tell me that you were preparing yourself to come with me if we come to Texas. May God not permit it, for it would be the most foolish thing you could do. You can't imagine how a woman who follows the troops, whether an officer or a private, is criticized. You can't imagine the work I as a man undergo, walking on foot all day and sleeping under a blanket which serves as a tent at night to serve as some protection, etc. Our food is ham and corn bread. I don't want to tell you anymore because I'd never end if I wrote all day. The only thing I implore you is that you never again think of coming where I am, because the soldier doesn't know how much time he's going to be in one place, and I don't have the means of having a Negro and a wagon and mules so that you could come to see and accompany me and if I had a million *pesos* I would not do it. I would never allow you to come see me unless we were camped in some part close to San Antonio such as Seguín, Tex. or Gonzales. Military life is the most miserable there is in this world. I'd rather be a Negro than [in the] military. A soldier or officer has to have a pass to leave one or two miles outside the camp and a Negro doesn't need a pass.

I was sick two or three days with a headache and leg and stomach pains. I believe it's the result of the soakings day and night and since I let my clothes dry on me, that's probably the reason. And since I don't have money even to buy good shoes and the ones I have are all torn and the mud and water goes right through, I think that's why I got sick. For almost two days, I had almost nothing to eat. I only drank water and had a bite of bread from time to time because already I don't even want to see the ham and corn bread; we eat it because we have nothing else. No, my darling, you can't imagine the sad life I'm leading. Yesterday I found seven lice on my clothes and it wasn't the first time, and it's all due to lack of money, and not only I but almost everyone of the soldiers and many of the officers. One of my officer friends was telling me that he had found four lice. Yes, my love, things have happened to me since I became a soldier which I never thought possible in this world. I don't want to tell you any more of what happens because you would be very sad. When I visit you one time, I'll tell you because the story is very long, but if my God permits me to survive this war, I'll first cut my neck than be drafted in another one. I had a good army tent but someone stole it and now we use a blanket as a tent and one gets soaked, clothes and all. Many times I've awakened and found myself in two inches of water under me, and it has rained two or three days and two or three nights without stopping. That's all for right now, the story is very long.

———◆◆◆◆———

Camp near Hempstead, Texas
May 15th of 1865

Dear Elenita:

Yesterday I received your very valued letter dated the 8th of the present [month] in which you tell me that you're waiting for me to tell you if I received the ten gold *pesos* which you sent me. Well I've already written you two or three letters in which I inform you that I received them but for you not to send me more money that way because there is great risk of losing it and it's best if you don't do it again. You tell me you've already received Jesus's things; well, the one who took them is a captain, but he's a man who's very hard with his soldiers, they can't see him. However, he's very good to me. You tell me that the 5th of the present [month] the Mexicans had a dance and that it was very beautiful. Well, I'm very happy if you enjoyed it which is the same as if I had been there by your side. What I want is for you to enjoy yourself and never be sad. I would've become very happy if I had been present by your side, there is nothing that would've given me more pleasure in this world, but I think that in a short time I should be by your side. Is my friend and school mate Jose Arizpe still in San Antonio?[71] If he is give him many greetings from me and tell him I'm very well.

I'm very sorry that the old lady, the mother of Mrs. Considerand already passed away. Well, my darling, there's nothing new here except that most of the troops on the other side of the Mississippi have surrendered and all the troops are very disconsolate and I fear that they will not fight well if we engage in a battle soon.

A few minutes ago Cresencio Navarro left.[72] He was here two or three hours with me and he ate here. I gave him a little ham and corn bread, this is the food of the Confederacy. He's a good youth, very fat and in very good health. I think that in four or six weeks we're going to know if the enemy is going to attack Laredo or not. As to when this war will end I believe it'll end this year, and I wouldn't be surprised if the enemy takes possession of this state. The troops are too disconsolate because of what happened on the other side of the Mississippi.

Write me soon and tell me all the news.

Kiss Lito and our daughter and you receive many more [kisses] from your affectionate husband,

Manuel

Greetings to all my relatives and acquaintances who ask about me.

Manuel Y

———◆◆◆◆◆———

Letter Fragment [1864?][73]

. . . after the long stop, as he wishes, knife, pistol or whatever he desires and at the hour he says, after the long stop, he sent word to me with his second, that he was very hurt over what has occurred, and that he took everything back except that I was a better man than he, than the fool he is, but that if I did not take that back that he was going to fight me. I sent word to him through his second that I did not take anything back and that I was ready to fight at anytime he wanted. Then his second, a lieutenant officer friend of mine, seeing that I was very determined to fight, said that he didn't want to be his second, and then Lieutenant Hafner said that he would look for another second. I immediately went and sought a second secretly, a very good officer friend, and he accepted to be my second but Lieutenant H[afner] repented upon seeing that I was very determined and that I was counting on my knowing how to handle arms much better than he. And if he had been a gentleman and man he would've challenged me as he had said he would after I didn't take anything back about what he said. So he had to swallow everything and keep quiet. He didn't speak to me for several days and afterwards he became a very good friend of mine and he kept speaking to me so that we are now as good friends as always, and we sleep in the same tent. Don't tell anyone about this and continue to be a friend of his wife as if you didn't know anything because he sought me out first. In a few days he'll become a first lieutenant; tomorrow he goes to be tested for first lieutenant.

I want you to tell me who told you about what happened to me with Lieutenant Hafner and Sergeant [Leandro] Bernal.[74] In your next letter I want you to tell me what you sent in my package and if you put my name and the regiment on top. My darling, on the last mail I sent you a paper for you to get firewood, but I don't think it's good, it was very dark and I couldn't see. But today I'm sending you two good ones to last you for two months.

Today I wrote a long letter to my *compadre* Y. Cassiano. If you find yourself in need, call him to help you and I'll pay back his favors if I get to return to S. A., since having relatives hasn't helped you because they never seem to do you any favors now that you need them most and your husband is absent.

Find out where Don Tomas Whitehead is and what command he belongs to so I can write him.[75] I want him to stop at the house when he returns so that he can help you with something you might need. Send me letter stamps if you can get them from Mr. [E. C.] Dewey because here we can't find any.[76] As to where Cresenciano Navarro is, he is at Black River about one hundred eighty miles from here. A soldier received a letter from his brother who is in the same company where Crecenciano of our company is. I'll write him a letter and then I'll be able to tell you better where he is. My dear, don't send me clothing. I now have plenty, the only thing I need are socks and handkerchiefs. I bought two pair of pants, a shirt and a pair of shorts. I have enough for this winter. I've just signed an application for Lieutenant Hafner to go to San Antonio. I believe he'll leave in a few days. Kiss Lito and our daughter and you receive many more from

> Your loving husband who desires
> more seeing you than writing,
> Manuel

Letter Fragment [1864][77]

. . . of the morning, and there was an order that there was only one wagon for each regiment so that all the officers and soldiers had to take all that they had on their backs with the exception of the mayor's staff. My friend McCormack took my coat in his trunk. Therefore many of us practically gave away many things which we could not take. I gave two pairs of underwear, a flannel shirt, two blue ones, and one blanket and I sold a pair of new boots almost given away because I sold them on credit for sixty *pesos* and they were worth about a hundred some and the same thing happened to many officers.

I'll be very happy if we don't go to the other side of the Mississippi River because this order has caused more than two hundred desertions in the division from what I have been told, but they have captured more

9. Elena and Manuel Yturri pose with nine of their ten children in San Antonio on their fiftieth wedding anniversary, April 14, 1910. Standing, from left to right: Robert Yturri, Elvira Alice Yturri, Mary Josephine James, Edward Yturri, Evelyn Yturri, Henry Yturri, and Fred Yturri. Seated, left to right: Elena "Leontine" Marx, Manuel and Elena, and Manuel Yturri III. Their tenth child, Alfred, had died earlier. Courtesy of John Yturri.

than a hundred. Most of them are handcuffed and shackled. Yesterday they placed a first lieutenant in our brigade [in the] guardhouse for having helped some escape, according to what I was told was the cause. I believe they will have to execute some of the deserters. But I do believe that if we're going to the other side many more will desert.

My friend McCormack and Martiniano Rodríguez send you many greetings. Lt. McCormack is going to send this letter enclosed in one for Capt. Lively by courier as official business he has with him & I think you will receive this soon. My dear, I am not tired of your complainings to me. I only am sorry that I am not by your side and you would not

10. Yturri family grave marker in Mission Burial Park No. 1, San Antonio. Photograph by Jerry Thompson.

11.   A prominent rancher and San Antonio public official, Manuel Yturri II outlived his brother-in-law by forty-eight years. Photograph by Jerry Thompson.

have troubled yourself so much as you have & particularly about the house. But I hope in your next you write me you tell me you are living in it.

How was it that you didn't place the furniture in your mother's home instead of having them out in the sun where they could crack or be put out of order?

My darling, you can't imagine what I would give to be by your side. I would gladly be a private in Texas only to see you and our two children again and be at home a month at your side. I would be satisfied to be a private during the war. Instead here we have a miserable life eating corn bread, coffee made from corn without sugar, meat barely once or twice a day, etc. I have no money, not even one cent and if I had it it wouldn't help because here you can't find anything.

Have you had to take anything from Lito's piggy bank? Not a single day goes by that I don't force Martiniano to tell me about you and Lito and our daughter. If you take money from the piggy bank write down

12.   Most of Capt. Manuel Yturri's letters were addressed to his wife, Elena. Mother of ten children, Elena de la Garza Yturri outlived her husband by twelve years, dying at the age of eighty-four in 1925. Photograph by Jerry Thompson.

what you take and is left for my curiosity and to know how much it is to repay Lito later.

If you can send me a pair of heavy work pants, not the dressy ones I have, with Capt. Lively send them or with a reliable person, if they can bring them for now.

Kiss Lito and our daughter and you receive many more. Ask for Eugenio Navarro's address, company, regiment, brigade and division so I can write him.

Say hello to all my relatives and acquaintances.

> Write Lieut. M. Yturri, 3rd, Lucketts
> Regt., Texas Vol. Infty.
> Waterhouse's Brigade, Walker's
> Division
> Shreveport, Louisiana

How much rent are you receiving each month? And your expenses? And your county, state, city and war taxes? Do you have enough to live well?

Yours until death,
Manuel Yturri
Mrs. Manuel Yturri
San Antonio
Texas

Appendix

This unpublished, anonymous poem is part of the privately held Yturri Papers. The poem was written in Spanish and is translated into English here by José Roberto Juárez and Sara Alicia Pompa.

On the Unfortunate Death	De la suerte desgraciada
Of an Honorable Gentleman	de un caballero de honor
Let the People Know	la gente viva avisaba
He Died Bravely	que murió por su valor
He enlisted enthusiastically	Entro tan de buena gana
As a Southern Captain	Como capitán sureño
And at the hands of the Northerners	Y por manos del norteño
He was killed in Louisiana	El fue muerto en la Luciana
Today most Mexicans	Hoy la gente mexicana
Find themselves grieving	La más se haya congojada
At seeing the poor fate	De ver la mala tanteada
Of a very young lad	De un joven de corta edad
Jesus Garza, whose luck	De Jesús Garzas es verdad
Was truly unfortunate.	De la suerte desgraciada
He was highly esteemed	Era hombre tan apreciado
By all his people	Para toda su nación
Today, the bullet from the barrel of a gun	Hoy la bala del cañon
His body has devoured	Su cuerpo le ha devorado
After cold bullets	Después de haberle pegado
Hit him directly	Balas frías a color
Yet with great fury	Pero con grande furor
He fought like a brave man	Entro como hombre valiente
I let all the people know	Notició a toda la gente
About a gentleman of honor.	De un caballero de honor

He was loved by all
For his way of life
All must surely feel [badly for]
What happened to him
Yet God has already been served
With his soul delivered
And he reached the end of his road
Jesus made him strong
He was killed by the Yankees
The people are informed.

Ultimately, it was God's decree
That he should die
The luck that he received
Was His will
He handed his soul to God
Fearless and willingly, of course
His relatives sorrowfully
Pray to him to my God
All pray, even those
He killed by his bravery.

Era de todos querido
Por su modo de vivir
A fuerza se ha de sentir
De haberle acontecido
Pero ya Diós fue servido
Que su alma fuera entregada
Y su raya fue llegada
Jesús que la hace tan fuerte
Los yanquis le dieron su muerte
La gente viva avisaba

En fin mi Dios decretó
Quitarlo de padecer
Fue por su propio querer
La suerte que le toco
A Diós el alma entregó
Por su propio gusto sin temor
Sus parientes con dolor
Ruegan por él a mi Diós
Todos dicen aún a los
Que murió por su valor

Notes

INTRODUCTION

1. Thompson, *Vaqueros in Blue and Gray,* 130–92.

2. *San Antonio Light,* Apr. 30, 1912. For an excellent study of Tejanos during the Mexican era, see Tijerina, *Tejanos & Texas under the Mexican Flag.* For equally superb studies of San Antonio during this same period, see de la Teja, *San Antonio de Béxar;* and Ramos, *Beyond the Alamo.* Helen Yturri tried unsuccessfully for several years to determine Joseph de la Garza's exact birth date and concluded that he was born sometime between February 1842 and November 1843. When enlisting in the 6th Infantry on March 31, 1862, however, de la Garza indicated that he was twenty-three.

3. Almaráz, *San Antonio Missions and Their System of Land Tenure,* 23, 39; *San Antonio Light,* Jan. 9, 13, 14, 17, 1976, Aug. 3, 1983, Feb. 1, 1989; *San Antonio News,* Jan. 12, 1976, Dec. 15, 1977; *San Antonio Express,* Jan. 9, 16, 1976, Jan. 30, 1977; *San Antonio Express News,* Feb. 27, 1994. Ben Milam and the Texans had camped at this "Old Mill" on December 4, 1835, before attacking the Mexican garrison in San Antonio. The noted San Antonio architect Alfred Giles redesigned the home at 327 South Presa in 1880. For the emergence of the Bexareño landholding elite, see Poyo, "Immigrants and Integration in Late Eighteenth-Century Béxar," 85–103.

4. Chabot, *Makers of San Antonio,* 80; Brown, "Story of San Antonio Money," 1463–69.

5. De la Teja, *Revolution Remembered.*

6. Slave Census, 1850, 1860, Bexar County, Tex., Record Group (hereafter RG) 29, National Archives, Washington, D.C. (hereafter NA)

7. J. B. Emig to Mariano Rodríguez, Oct. 21, 1852, Yturri Papers, private collection; Buckley, *When Jesuits Were Giants,* 252–53. The records of St. Joseph's College, including correspondence, ledgers, reports, and assorted papers, can be found in the archives of the University of Notre Dame at South Bend, Indiana. Unfortunately, the records from 1844 to 1869, covering the period that Yturri and other young men from San Antonio would have attended the college, have been lost.

8. *San Antonio Weekly Alamo Express,* Feb. 11, 13, 1861.

9. Thompson, *Civil War in the Southwest,* xv; Theophilus Noel, *A*

Campaign from Santa Fe to the Mississippi, Being a History of the Old Sibley Brigade from its First Organization to the Present Time: Its Campaigns in New Mexico, Arizona, Texas, Louisiana, and Arkansas in the Years 1861–2–3–4, ed. Martin Hardwick Hall and Edwin Adams Davis (1865; reprint, Houston: Stagecoach, 1964), 13; *San Antonio Semi-Weekly News,* May 22, 1862.

10. Joseph de la Garza Compiled Service Record, Confederate Adjutant General's Office, RG 109, NA (hereafter CSR); *San Antonio Semi-Weekly News,* Jan. 2, Mar. 7, 1862. At the time of his death, Captain de la Garza was serving in the 17th Consolidated Regiment of Texas Infantry and Dismounted Cavalry. This regiment had been formed in July 1863 from men of the 15th, 17th, 18th, 24th, and 25th regiments of cavalry and the 6th and 10th regiments of infantry who had not been captured at Arkansas Post, Arkansas, on January 11, 1863.

11. Manuel Yturri CSR. Yturri was paroled at San Antonio on August 12, 1865.

12. SO No. 231, Aug. 27, 1863, *War of the Rebellion,* ser. 1, 26(2):183–84; SO, June 9, 1862, ibid. For the regiment's service at Galveston and the mouth of the Brazos River at Velasco, see SO No. 325, Nov. 29, 1863, ibid., 456–57; and GO No. 217, Dec. 15, 1863, ibid., 509–10. Although desertions in the 3rd Texas Infantry had proven to be a constant problem along the Rio Grande, it was not until the summer of 1863 on Galveston Island that service grew particularly unpleasant in the heat and humidity as rations grew progressively bad. Then, as conditions continued to deteriorate, the men refused to drill until things improved. After spending three years along the Rio Grande and the Texas coast, in March 1864 the 3rd Texas was ordered to Louisiana to join Maj. Gen. John G. Walker's division near Shreveport. Arriving too late for the battles of Mansfield and Pleasant Hill, the regiment was sent to Arkansas with Brig. Gen. William R. Scurry's brigade and were, as Yturri vividly writes, at the bloody Battle of Jenkins' Ferry on April 30, 1864. Returning to Louisiana, they remained with Walker's Texas Division until the end of the war. Yturri was at Camp Groce near Hempstead when Walker's Division disbanded in late May 1865.

13. Angel Navarro to Santiago Vidaurri, Dec. 1, 1863, Correspondencia de Santiago Vidaurri, Archivo General del Estado de Nuevo León, Monterrey, Mexico. Navarro served in the Texas legislature before the war and helped raise and command Company H of Col. Alfred Marmaduke Hobby's 8th Texas Infantry on the Rio Grande frontier and in Atascosa County. Tired of the discrimination that plagued Tejanos in Confederate

service, he departed for Mexico in late 1863, though returning to his large ranch southwest of San Antonio by 1869. Navarro later moved to Laredo, where he became city attorney and deeply involved in local politics before his assassination in the summer of 1876 by a "murderous villain" who fled to Mexico. Helen P. Trimpi to Jerry Thompson, containing entry on Navarro in forthcoming *Crimson Confederates: Harvard Men who Fought for the South*, Nov. 10, 2007, in editor's possession. See also Camilla Campbell, "José Ángel Navarro," *Handbook of Texas* Online, http://www.tshaonline .org/handbook/online/articles/NN/fna8.html (accessed Nov. 20, 2006); Navarro CSR; and *San Antonio Daily Express*, Aug. 11, 1876. For José Antonio Navarro, see McDonald and Matovina, *Defending Mexican Valor in Texas*.

14.   Pronunciamiento, Antonio Abad Dias, Apr. 17, 1865, Cecilio Vela Papers, private collection; Antonio Garza to Josefa de la Garza, Apr. 11, Aug. 2, 1864, De la Garza Papers, Library of the Daughters of the Republic of Texas at the Alamo, San Antonio. The Confederate government passed a controversial conscription act in April 1862. All "white men" between the ages of eighteen and thirty-five, excepting those holding positions in government, industry, transportation, education, or other occupations considered vital to the war effort, were subject to the draft. After considerable hesitation, Gov. Francis R. Lubbock agreed to comply with the law. Five months later another conscript act was passed, raising the age of draftees to forty-five. Later yet, men as young as seventeen and as old as fifty were included as potential draftees. Without hesitation, state conscription agents were ordered into South Texas to draft Mexican Texans. Evasion and resistance followed. Upon nearing San Antonio, Tejano and Mexicano teamsters were said to have driven their wagons around rather than through the city for fear of being drafted. Thompson, *Vaqueros in Blue and Gray*, 56, 57.

15.   Several letters from Union Tejanos, including those of Capt. Cecilio Vela, have recently surfaced in private family archives. Manuel Flores to Jerry Thompson, Aug. 19, 20, 2009, e-mail messages in editor's possession.

16.   *San Antonio Express*, Feb. 26, 27, 1913; Twelfth Census, 1900, Bexar County, Tex., N.A.

PART I. LETTERS OF CAPT. JOSEPH DE LA GARZA

1.   Camp Henry E. McCulloch was established by Maj. Alexander M. Haskell four miles north of Victoria and was named for the commander of the Department of Texas. It was here, as de la Garza indicates, that the

first companies of the 6th Texas Infantry were mustered into Confederate service.

2. Salado Creek rises in northern Bexar County and flows southeast thirty-eight miles into the San Antonio River, about five miles southeast of the city. The Battle of Rosalis (1813) and the Battle of Salado (1842) were fought along the banks of the creek.

3. On the east bank of the Colorado River, three miles east of Columbus, and along the Texas and New Orleans Railroad, Alleyton flourished during the Civil War. It was also the terminus of the Buffalo Bayou, Brazos, and Colorado Railroad, which had been completed in 1860, and the beginning of the "cotton road" by which wagon trains carried cotton across Texas to the Rio Grande at Brownsville, Rio Grande City, Laredo, and Eagle Pass before proceeding into Mexico. For a time Alleyton was the largest town in Colorado County. "Alleyton, Texas," *Handbook of Texas* Online, http://www.tshaonline.org/handbook/online/articles/AA/hna25_print.html (accessed Jan. 2, 2008).

4. Only nineteen at the time and a close friend of Captain de la Garza, Pedro Ville Sarats (Sarate or Zarate) enlisted in the Alamo Guards in San Antonio and was promoted to fourth corporal in Company K, 6th Texas Infantry on December 14, 1862. Taken prisoner at Arkansas Post on January 11, 1863, he was held at Camp Butler at Springfield, Illinois, before being exchanged. After rejoining his company, he deserted in March 1864. Sarats Compiled Service Record, Confederate Adjutant General's Office, RG 109, NA (hereafter CSR); Spurlin, *Diary of Charles A. Leuschner*, 98.

5. Eugenio Navarro, twenty-two, is listed in the Alamo Guards (Company K, 6th Texas Infantry) on March 31, 1862, as first corporal. His service record indicates that he was five feet, five inches in height, with dark eyes, dark hair, and a dark complexion. Taken prisoner at Arkansas Post on January 11, 1863, he was imprisoned at Camp Butler, at Springfield, Illinois. After being exchanged, he was elected second lieutenant on March 9, 1864, at Dalton, Georgia, then promoted first lieutenant a month later. Navarro was captured at the bloody Battle of Franklin, Tennessee, on November 30, 1864 and held first at Nashville, then at the military prison in Louisville, Kentucky, before finally being transferred to Johnson's Island in Lake Erie at Sandusky, Ohio. After taking the oath of allegiance on June 17, 1865, he was released and returned to San Antonio. Navarro is enumerated on the 1870 census as a clerk with a wife and two children. Navarro CSR; Spurlin, *Diary of Charles A. Leuschner*, 96; Ninth Census, 1870, Bexar County, Tex.; Tenth Census, 1880, Atascosa County, Tex.

6. After departing Camp McCullouch and spending several days in camp near Eagle Lake, the 6th Texas Infantry arrived at Camp No. 25 near Tyler on June 24, 1862. They departed on July 1 for Little Rock, Arkansas. Regimental Returns, 6th Texas Infantry, CAGO, RG 109, NA (hereafter RR, by regiment). Much of this information is also available in the 6th Texas Infantry CSRs.

7. Elena refers to María Elena de la Trinidad de la Garza, Captain de la Garza's older sister and the wife of Capt. Manuel Yturri. Born on May 30, 1841, the daughter of José Antonio de la Garza and María Josefa Menchaca, she married Yturri on April 25, 1860, and together they would have ten children. Twelve years after her husband's death, Elena died on July 31, 1925. Rodríguez, *Memoirs of Early Texas,* 66; Chabot, *Makers of San Antonio,* 226; Elena Yturri tombstone, St. Mary's Cemetery, San Antonio, Tex.

8. Younger brother of Captain de la Garza, José Leonardo was born on August 5, 1844, the tenth and youngest child of José Antonio de la Garza and María Josefa Menchaca. Leonardo was attending Williams College, at Williamstown in the Berkshires of northwestern Massachusetts, when the war erupted. After his funds were exhausted, he taught school in Philadelphia and in 1864 joined the U.S. Navy as a surgeon's assistant. Eventually completing his education at Williams College, and after an eleven-year absence, the articulate and well-read young man returned to San Antonio in November 1865. He married Carolina Callahan at Ursuline Convent three years later, and from the marriage sixteen children were born, eleven of whom survived to adulthood. In time de la Garza became a leading banker and businessman in San Antonio, wrote an autobiography, and built a large home on Broadway and North Alamo streets. Leonardo de la Garza died on September 17, 1923. Many of his letters to his mother and relatives in San Antonio, written from Falmouth, Smith College, New York, and from Philadelphia before and during the Civil War, have survived. José Leonardo de la Garza Baptismal Certificate, Aug. 11, 1844, Catholic Archives of San Antonio (courtesy of Helen Yturri). See also Leonardo de la Garza tombstone, San Fernando No. 1 Cemetery, San Antonio; and Leonardo de la Garza Letters, 1857–65, private collection of Helen and John Yturri.

9. On July 24, 1862, the 6th Texas arrived at Camp No. 46 at Rockport, Arkansas, a few miles north of Malvern and about eighteen miles east of Hot Springs. RR, 6th Texas Infantry.

10. Born in Danville, Boyle County, Kentucky, in 1831, McAllister came to San Antonio as a teenager in 1847 to enter commercial life. McAllister's

Rangers were first enlisted for six months and incorporated into Lt. Col. John Robert Baylor's 2nd Texas Mounted Rifles as Company A. In the summer of 1861, they helped occupy the Mesilla Valley in southern New Mexico Territory, or what the Confederates came to call the Territory of Arizona. On August 7, upon the expiration of their terms of service, McAllister and most of his men returned to San Antonio. McAllister announced in the *San Antonio Semi-Weekly News* in early January 1862 that he was raising an infantry company for "coast defense." He went on to command Company K (Alamo Rifles), 6th Texas Infantry but was dropped from the rolls on November 28, 1863. After the war McAllister served two terms as alderman in San Antonio. Chabot, *Makers of San Antonio,* 404; Spurlin, *Diary of Charles A. Leuschner,* 96; Thompson, *From Desert to Bayou,* 8–10, 27, 72, 103, 105; *San Antonio Semi-Weekly News,* Jan. 2, 1862.

11. Upstream from Mission San Francisco de la Espada, the fields along the west bank of the San Antonio River were watered by an acequia that included the oldest stone aqueduct in Texas. Constructed in 1731, the irrigation system fed fields of corn, beans, squash, cotton, and sugarcane. Cox, *Spanish Acequias of San Antonio,* 30–34.

12. José Antonio de la Garza married Gertrudis Rivas in 1813; following her death, he wed María Josefa Menchaca in 1824. Chabot, *Makers of San Antonio,* 78–79; Helen Yturri, interview with editor, Sept. 26, 2007.

13. This may be George P. Finlay, who was elected captain of Company H, 6th Texas Infantry. Thirty-two years old and six feet, four inches in height, Finlay was arrested for unknown reasons and then declared absent without leave in June 1863, mistakenly as it turned out, before the Confederate surrender at Arkansas Post on January 11, 1863. After being held at Camp Chase, at Columbus, Ohio, Finlay and his men were exchanged at City Point, Virginia, on April 29. Finlay CSR; Spurlin, *Diary of Charles A. Leuschner,* 90. Much of the data in the service records of the 6th Texas Infantry has been carefully compiled by Spurlin as an appendix to the Leuschner diary.

14. At the age of twenty-one, Joseph A. Costa enrolled in Company G, 6th Texas Infantry as third sergeant at Austin, Texas, on October 1, 1861. Promoted to second sergeant, he was reported sick at Arkansas Post in December 1862 and was presumed to have been killed or taken prisoner during the Federal siege and attack in January 1863. As it turned out, Costa was able to escape and later rejoined his regiment. Costa CSR.

15. At age twenty-two, Antonio Bustillos enlisted in the 6th Texas Infantry at San Antonio on April 17, 1862. He was ill when captured at

Arkansas Post on January 11, 1863. Later in camp at Dalton, Georgia, in March 1864, Bustillos wrote his mother of "awaiting the enemy's advance" and praying "that this bloody war should be over by year's end." During the siege of Atlanta, he wrote again that his brigade had lost 440 men in the war, 102 of them in the furious fighting in Georgia. Bustillos was convinced that Maj. Gen. William T. Sherman's continued advance would end the war. Wounded at Jonesboro, south of Atlanta, on September 1, 1864, he was exchanged and then listed in ill health at the "Texas Hospital" at Auburn, Alabama. Bustillos recovered and was present when Gen. Joseph E. Johnston surrendered to Sherman at Durham Station, North Carolina, on April 26, 1865. Antonio Bustillos to My Dear Mother, Mar. 1, 1864 (quote), De la Garza Papers, Library of the Daughters of the Republic of Texas at the Alamo; Bustillos to Trinidad Bustillos de [la] Garza, Aug. 15, 1864, ibid. See also Bustillos CSR.

At age twenty-three, Antonio Zuñiga (Suniga) too was taken prisoner at Arkansas Post. He died at Camp Butler, Illinois, on May 8, 1863. Zuñiga CSR.

Thirty-nine years of age, Garza enlisted at San Antonio as a private in the Alamo Guards, and like most men in the regiment, he was captured at Arkansas Post on January 11, 1863. Imprisoned at Camp Butler, Illinois, he was exchanged only to be wounded at the Battle of Franklin on November 20, 1864. Garza CSR.

16. Individuals listed here represent many of the leading families of San Antonio and the in-laws of the Yturris and de la Garzas.

Through the years, the Cassianos emerged as one of the more prominent families in San Antonio's social and economic life. Born at San Remo, Italy, in 1791, following the War of 1812, José Cassiano made his way to New Orleans, where he became a successful merchant and property owner. Not long after Mexico gained its independence from Spain in 1821, he moved to San Antonio, where he acquired extensive property. During the Texas Revolution, he spied on Antonio López de Santa Anna and the Mexican Army and helped finance the Texas cause. Cassiano extended hospitality to the Americans in the early days of the Republic of Texas and was three times elected alderman in San Antonio. He died on January 1, 1862, seven months after de la Garza's letter, and was buried in San Fernando Cemetery. De la Garza and Manuel Yturri were friends with the Cassiano children, including thirty-one-year-old Ignacio, who had enlisted as a private in Company A, 33rd Texas Cavalry (James Duff's Partisan Rangers) but was discharged in September 1862 when he hired Jesus Garza as a substitute.

On the eve of the war, Ignacio and Mary Cassiano were parents of seven children, ages two to fourteen. Ignacio was a "house renter" in San Antonio with real estate of $10,000. Twenty-five-year-old Simon Cassiano also enrolled in the 33rd Texas Cavalry and served in Capt. Refugio Benavides's company at Ringgold Barracks and Carrizo (Zapata). Eighth Census, 1860, Wilson County, Bexar County, Tex.; Chabot, *Makers of San Antonio*, 223; Ignacio Cassiano CSR; Simon Cassiano CSR.

    Ed Rivas, twenty-four, is listed on the 1860 census as a wagoner at San Antonio with no real or personal property. Eighth Census, 1860, Bexar County, Tex. The individual may have been later enumerated as Edward Rivas, laborer, age fifty-four, with real estate of $4,000. Ninth Census, 1870, Bexar County, Tex.

    In 1860, Louisiana-born Ernest B. Edmunds, twenty-six and single, is listed in San Antonio's First Ward as a merchant. A year later at Concepción Mission, he married Manuel Yturri's younger and favorite sister, María Josefa Vicenta Carmen, on August 1. Five children were born of the marriage. Edmunds was born on August 10, 1840, and died on April 20, 1870; Vicenta was born on July 19, 1841, and died on June 6, 1924. First educated at Ursuline Convent in San Antonio, she was sent to Ursuline Convent in New Orleans, one of the top schools for young women at the time, and excelled in music and languages. Somewhat of a Greek and Latin scholar, she was also fluent in French, Spanish, and English, graduating in 1861. According to family legend, the couple met while Vicenta was in school in New Orleans. Chabot, *Makers of San Antonio*, 223; Eighth Census, 1860, Bexar County, Tex.; tombstone inscriptions, Mission Burial Park No. 1, San Antonio.

    For the Rodríguez family in San Antonio, see Chabot, *Makers of San Antonio*, 170–74; and Rodríguez, *Memoirs of Early Texas*, 43–51. For the Lockmars, see n. 24.

    17.   Joseph Rafael's older sister, Carolina, was married to Philadelphia-born Bart DeWitt. Chabot, *Makers of San Antonio*, 79; Rodríguez, *Memoirs of Early Texas*, 59; Joe DeWitt, interview with editor, Jan. 2, 2008. See also n. 26.

    18.   Joseph Rafael de la Garza's older sister, Margarita, married Virginia-born James L. Trueheart, on February 15, 1848. The thirty-six-year-old, Virginia-born Trueheart is listed on the 1860 Bexar County census along with Margarita, age twenty-nine, and their three children. He served briefly as a city alderman in 1841 and in August 1863 enlisted in Company A, 30th Texas State Troops, a "reserve corps" of Confederate cavalry organized at

San Pedro Springs. Trueheart died at the age of sixty-seven on November 30, 1882. Margarita died of dengue fever at the age of sixty-eight on October 12, 1898. Eighth Census, 1860, Bexar County, Tex.; tombstones, St. Fernando No. 1 Cemetery, San Antonio; Chabot, *Makers of San Antonio,* 79; Rodríguez, *Memoirs of Early Texas,* 55; Trueheart CSR; *San Antonio Semi-Weekly News,* Aug. 27, 1863.

19. Kentucky-born John Carroll Crawford, a Kentucky miller, married Josefina de la Garza, the older sister of Joseph de la Garza, in San Antonio on December 10, 1849. They are enumerated on the 1860 San Antonio census with four children and personal property of $4,000. Eighth Census, 1860, Bexar County, Tex.; Chabot, *Makers of San Antonio,* 79; Marriage Book B (1848–52), County Clerk's Office, Bexar County, Tex.

20. Robert B. Harvey, age thirty-three, was a first lieutenant in Company H, 6th Texas Infantry and was said to have been "regularly elected by his men." The company was composed of recruits from Calhoun and Victoria counties. Following the Confederate surrender at Arkansas Post, the prisoners, including Harvey, were taken up the Mississippi River on steamboats and then transferred directly to railroad cars for the journey to Camp Chase, Columbus, Ohio. Six feet in height, with blue eyes and a light complexion, Harvey was transferred to Fort Delaware, in the Delaware River south of New Castle, Delaware, before being exchanged at City Point, Virginia. He was killed at the Battle of Chickamauga on September 20, 1863. Spurlin, *Diary of Charles A. Leuschner,* 90.

21. In the summer of 1862, intent on helping drive the Confederates out of New Mexico Territory, the uncompromising and ruthless Brig. Gen. James H. Carleton led 2,350 men (fifteen infantry companies, five cavalry companies, and an artillery battery) east along the Gila Trail through the Sonoran Desert, or what the men called the "Great Desert," in 120-degree heat and the worst drought in thirty years. By August Carleton had successfully occupied the southern half of New Mexico Territory and Fort Bliss, in far western Texas. For Carleton and the California Column, see Hunt, *Army of the Pacific;* Hunt, *Major General James H. Carleton;* Miller, *Confederate Column in New Mexico;* Masich, *Civil War in Arizona;* and Jerry Thompson, ed., *Civil War in New Mexico Territory: Wallen and Evans Inspection Reports, 1862–1863* (Albuquerque: University of New Mexico Press, 2008).

22. The *San Antonio Herald* grew out of the *San Antonio Alamo Star,* a newspaper established in 1854 by James Pearson Newcomb. With the help of J. M. West, Newcomb began a weekly newspaper called the *San Antonio*

Herald on April 3, 1855. In 1856 John D. Logan and S. C. Thompson purchased the paper and in 1857 began publishing a daily. The *Herald* was published as a daily, weekly, and tri-weekly from 1858 until 1880, when it merged with the *San Antonio Daily Times.* Sibley, *Lone Stars and State,* 216–17, 251–52, 294–98. Frances Donecker, "San Antonio *Herald*," *Handbook of Texas* Online, http://www.tshaonline.org/handbook/online/articles/SS/ees4 .html (accessed Dec. 24, 2007).

23. This would have been the bloody and epic Seven Days Battle outside Richmond, Virginia, in the summer of 1862, during which the newly appointed commander of the Army of Northern Virginia, Robert E. Lee, drove the Army of the Potomac from the gates of the Confederate capital to the banks of the James River.

24. Said to have been "one of the reigning belles in the society circles of the town, made so by her great beauty and charm and her many accomplishments," Rudecinda, Captain de la Garza's older sister, became Sister Magdalena, Mother Superior of Ursuline Convent in San Antonio. One of the convent's founders in 1851, she entered the religious order two years later and supervised the education of hundreds of young women. She died on September 11, 1897, at the age of seventy-two. "Her talents, virtue, and earnest zeal for her work" won her "high commendation from the church dignitaries." Chabot, *Makers of San Antonio,* 79; Rodríguez, *Memoirs of Early Texas,* 55; newspaper clipping, Sept. 14, 1897, typescript (courtesy of Helen Yturri); Espuela, Sept. 11, 1897, Rev. Mother St. M. Magdalen (courtesy of Helen Yturri).

Since both Joseph de la Garza and Manuel Yturri were known to be close to the Seguín family, Erasmo is likely José Erasmo, brother of Juan Nepomuceno Seguín and the son of Erasmo Seguín, both of Texas Revolution fame. Fermín cannot be identified with certainty. Miguel García does not appear on the 1860 Bexar County census.

Anton Lockmars and María Apolinaria Treviño were parents of five children, Ysabel, Catarina Augusta, George, Adelina, and Pauline. A Croatian by birth, Lockmars came to Texas as part of John Charles Beales's Dolores Colony, which settled on Las Moros Creek near what is today Spofford. Threatened and attacked by Comanches, members of the colony fled to San Antonio in 1836. After marrying María Treviño in 1839, Lockmars served briefly as alderman in 1841 and opened a hotel in 1844 on Soledad Street. He was also part owner of the Bowie Tavern on Commerce Street and owned 1,476 acres of land along León Creek. After her husband died in 1848, María married Francois P. Giraud and became the mother of four additional children. She died in San Antonio on September 19, 1885; Manuel Yturri was one of the pallbearers at her funeral. *San Antonio Express*, Nov. 21, 1932; Chabot, *Makers of San Antonio*, 12–33; "Hotel Register Turns the Pages Back to Days of 1845 in San Antonio," Marmion Family Tree, http:// www.marmionfamilytree.com/SAExpress.html (accessed Jan. 3, 2008).

Born in 1846, Margarita Isidra Navarro was the daughter of José Antonio Navarro and Juana Chávez. She married Robert Langston; the couple became the parents of six children. Chabot, *Makers of San Antonio*, 205.

25. Annetta Magoffin was the daughter of prominent Santa Fe trader and El Paso secessionist James Wiley Magoffin and his wife, María Gertrudis Valdez de Veramendi. In San Antonio she married Joseph M. Dwyer, son of Edward Dwyer and Marianna Leal Ramón. In 1860 Dwyer was a "law student" in the city, living with his widowed mother and grandmother. He became a prominent merchant and landowner, rose to be a leader in the Bexar County Democratic Party, and was selected as a delegate to the Democratic convention that nominated Samuel J. Tilden for president in 1876; he also served as alderman in San Antonio from1882 to 1884. In 1900 Annie Dwyer was living on South Flores Street with her daughter, Annette, and her son-in-law, George Schmitt. Eighth (1860), Tenth (1880), and Twelfth (1900) Censuses, Bexar County, Tex.; Green, *Place Names of San Antonio*, 10; Carol E. Christian, "Thomas B. Dwyer," *Handbook of Texas* Online, http://www.tshaonline.org/handbook/online/articles/DD/fdw2.html (accessed Dec. 16, 2007).

26. In 1860 the thirty-three-year-old Bartholomew Joseph DeWitt was the sutler at Fort McIntosh near Laredo, Texas. At the same time he held the hay and corn contracts for Fort Hudson and Fort Quitman in far West Texas. Born in either Maryland or Pennsylvania, DeWitt came to Texas after the war with Mexico and settled in San Antonio, where he married Carolina Angela de la Garza, the sister of Joseph de la Garza. In 1860 he is listed on the census at Fort Quitman, where he was rooming with the noted Texas frontiersman John Woodland. At the time DeWitt listed real estate of $1,300 and personal property of $5,000. Mother of five children, Carolina died unexpectedly in San Antonio in 1866, perhaps during the cholera epidemic that swept the city. Leaving his daughter Katie with the Sisters of Charity in the city and her younger siblings to be raised by relatives, DeWitt moved to Fort Concho shortly after the post was established in 1867. There he opened a mercantile business on the north bank of the North Concho River and named the settlement of gambling houses, saloons, and trading posts "Santa Angela" in honor of his deceased wife. Unfamiliar with Span-

ish, local residents corrupted the name to San Angela, and the town's first post office was established under that name in 1881. In 1883 federal officials changed the name of the community to San Angelo. Encountering financial difficulties, DeWitt returned to San Antonio, where he died in 1878. Today an idealistic and somewhat stereotypical sculpture of Carolina Angela de la Garza DeWitt overlooks the North Concho River at the San Angelo Visitors Center. Eighth Census, 1860, El Paso County, Tex.; Ninth Census, 1870, Bexar County, Tex.; Haley, *Fort Concho and the Texas Frontier,* 272, 290; Smith, *U.S. Army and the Texas Frontier Economy,* 206; Thompson, *Texas and New Mexico on the Eve of the Civil War,* 149.

27. This is likely George H. Sweet, fire-eating editor of the *San Antonio Herald*. Although various sources, including the *Handbook of Texas,* indicate his birthplace as Ulster County, New York, the 1860 Bexar County census enumerator listed him as having been born in New Brunswick, Canada, about 1818. The census, however, erroneously lists him as mayor of San Antonio; his brother, James R. Sweet, was mayor at the time. (For James R. Sweet, see part 2, n. 2.) George Sweet participated in the Mexican War and in the 1850s came to San Antonio, where he replaced James P. Newcomb as editor of the *Herald*. Noted for his sensational journalism, Sweet was elected captain of Company A, 15th Texas Cavalry on January 1, 1862, then colonel of the regiment three months later. Sweet and most of his men were captured at Arkansas Post but exchanged shortly thereafter, whereupon the colonel was sent to organize the men of his regiment who had managed to avoid capture. In 1864 he was ordered to Tyler and given command of Camp Ford, the largest Confederate prisoner of war camp west of the Mississippi River. Sweet later published *Texas: Her Early History, Climate, Soil, and Material Resources* as well as the *Texas New Yorker,* a monthly publication designed to promote interest in the Lone Star State. In 1878 he moved to Galveston, where he became publisher of the *Galveston Journal.* "George H. Sweet," *Handbook of Texas* Online, http://www.tshaonline.org/hanbook/online/articles/SS/fsw10.html (accessed Dec. 24, 2008); Sibley, *Lone Stars and State Gazettes,* 294–95; Sweet CSR; Eighth Census, 1860, Bexar County, Tex.

28. Father Giraudon first appears in the records of the Diocese of Galveston at San Antonio in 1855. He is mentioned again in 1859 as having jurisdiction over San José, San Juan Capistrano, San Francisco de la Espada, and the chapel of El Carmen at Medina. Almaráz, "French-Flavored Frontier"; Vertical File Directories, Diocese of Galveston, 1852–95, Catholic Archives of San Antonio, 214 (records courtesy of Félix D. Almaráz Jr.).

29. Thomas J. Churchill was born in Kentucky in 1824, educated at

St. Mary's College at Bardstown and at Transylvania University at Lexington. After serving in the Mexican War, he moved to Arkansas and in 1861 was postmaster at Little Rock. After raising a Confederate regiment and seeing action at Pea Ridge, Arkansas, he was promoted to brigadier general and fought in Kentucky. By December 1862 he was placed in command of Fort Hindman at Arkansas Post. Taken prisoner and exchanged, Churchill was blamed for the surrender, sent back to the Trans-Mississippi, and assigned to command troops from Texas. Many of the Texans protested, however, and some refused to serve under their new general. Placed in charge of Arkansas troops during the Red River Campaign, Churchill performed admirably and was promoted to major general in April 1864. After the war he was elected governor of Arkansas and died at Little Rock in 1905. Bailey, *Between the Enemy and Texas*, 95–106; Bailey, "Thomas James Churchill," 3:311; Warner, *Generals in Gray*, 49–50.

30. A large powder mill was located at Monumental and Commerce streets in San Antonio. With powder and lead from Mexico, the factory produced as many as 120,000 cartridges a month. A workroom near the mill, housing 1,500 pounds of powder, blew up in late June 1863, killing two workers, Ernst Guenther and Ignacio Salinas. *San Antonio Semi-Weekly Herald,* July 2, 1863; Winsor, *Texas in the Confederacy,* 43, 56. The powder mill is not mentioned in Nichols, *Quartermaster in the Trans-Mississippi.*

31. This is probably the gristmill that was powered by the waters of the Pajalache, or Concepción Acequia, and constructed by Manuel Yturri's father in 1820. Reconstruction of the mill was completed in May 1972 after Ernestine E. Edmunds, granddaughter of Manuel Yturri II, willed the property to the San Antonio Conservation Society.

32. Horatio Stephenson may be Lt. H. Stevenson of the 19th Texas Cavalry, who resigned from the army on May 6, 1863. A Horatio Stephenson (or Stevenson) is not listed on the Eighth or Ninth Texas Census or in other military records. "Record of Events for Nineteenth Texas Cavalry," *Supplement to the Official Records,* 68(2):105.

33. Vicente Martinez, twenty-three, served in Samuel D. Ragsdale's Battalion of Cavalry. Martinez CSR.

34. José Antonio "George" Navarro was the son of José Antonio Navarro of Texas Revolution and Republic of Texas fame and the brother of Sixto Eusebio and José Ángel, both of whom were officers and teenage friends of de la Garza and Yturri. The tombstone for Sixto Eusebio Navarro indicates that he died at the age of seventy-two on February 28, 1905. Chabot, *Makers of San Antonio,* 205.

Carlos Sandoval enlisted in Capt. Lorenzo Treviño's Company of Partisan Rangers and served as first corporal. He is probably the same Carlos Sandoval listed in the 1860 Bexar County census as married with a wife and five children and a farmer with personal property of $150. By 1870 he was still farming along the San Antonio River near Mission San José. Sandoval CSR; Eighth (1860) and Ninth (1870) Censuses, Bexar County, Tex. Antonio Garza cannot be identified with certainty.

35. John J. McCowan (or McCown or McCowen), twenty-nine, was elected captain of what became Company H, 15th Texas Cavalry at Clarksville in March 1862. He is certainly the same J. J. McCowan listed on the 1860 Fannin County census as a farmer living near the village of Sadonia with real estate of $600 and personal property of $400. Taken prisoner with his company at Arkansas Post on January 11, 1863, McCowan was reported missing from Camp Douglas, Illinois, and was not among the 520 prisoners and "one Negro Boy" exchanged at City Point, Virginia, on April 10. Although dropped from the rolls of the 15th Cavalry on December 6, 1864, he appears to be the same John J. McCown who later served in the 17th Consolidated Regiment and commanded the regiment during the last months of the war. About May 24, 1864, several companies of the 15th Cavalry were temporarily consolidated with the 6th and 10th Texas Infantry and later surrendered at Greensboro, North Carolina, on May 1, 1865. Portions of the 15th Texas Cavalry that remained west of the Mississippi River were also reorganized late in the war. Eighth Census, 1860, Fannin County, Tex.; McCowan CSR.

36. On the west bank of the Red River four miles north of Natchitoches, Grand Ecore was where the old Camino Real began its long track through the piney woods of northwestern Louisiana and Texas, then to San Antonio de Bexar, across the Rio Grande, and eventually to Mexico City. Prior to the Civil War, it had become a major steamboat landing and served as the port for the town of Natchitoches. During the Mexican War, the U.S. Army built two forts, Seldon and Solubrity, atop the 120-foot-high bluffs there. During the Civil War, the Confederates fortified these heights but abandoned them when Maj. Gen. Nathaniel P. Banks pushed his army upriver toward Shreveport during the Red River Campaign. Following the Union reversal at Mansfield and retreat from Pleasant Hill, Banks temporarily established his headquarters at Grand Ecore but evacuated the hamlet as the retreating Federals torched the few buildings and Dr. John Sibley's plantation. Joiner, *Blunder from Beginning to End*, 15–16, 20–22, 68–70, 151.

37. Called the "Greyhounds of the Mississippi," Maj. Gen. John G.

Walker's infantry division was the largest body of Texans, about 12,000 men, to serve in the Civil War. Created in 1862, the division fought at Mansfield, Pleasant Hill, and Jenkins' Ferry during the 1864 Red River Campaign. Lowe, *Walker's Texas Division.*

38. Composed of 1,500 men and forming part of Walker's Texas Division, Brig. Gen. Henry Eustace McCulloch's brigade saw extensive action during the Red River Campaign. McCulloch was the brother of Brig. Gen. Benjamin McCulloch, who was killed at the Battle of Pea Ridge, Arkansas, on March 7, 1862.

Although not possessing a military education and suffering from rheumatoid arthritis, Richard Taylor served with distinction under "Stonewall" Jackson in Virginia's Shenandoah Valley early in the war. He is best remembered, however, for his defense of southern Louisiana during the 1863 Bayou Teche Campaign as well as his defeat of Federal forces at Mansfield on April 8, 1864, during the Red River Campaign. Although thrown back at Pleasant Hill, Taylor nevertheless succeeded in forcing the Federals to withdraw. The son of Pres. Zachary Taylor, Richard Taylor rose to the rank of lieutenant general during the war and surrendered the last organized Confederate force east of the Mississippi in 1865. His reminiscence of the conflict, *Destruction and Reconstruction,* is considered the best account by any Confederate leader. T. Michael Parrish, *Richard Taylor: Soldier Prince of Dixie* (Chapel Hill: University of North Carolina Press, 1992).

39. C. R. Harrison, fifty-five, and his wife, Francis, are listed on the 1860 census at Shreveport. Harrison had migrated to Shreveport, where he acquired slaves and land valued at $15,000. Eighth Census, 1860, Caddo Parish, La.

Four Mile Spring was a favorite Confederate staging area on the Red River near Shreveport. In November 1863 the site was described by a Union prisoner of war as an "ice-bound" and "bleak" camp consisting of little more than a few "exposed dwellings." Federal prisoners were frequently held there before they were exchanged and sent downriver by steamboat.

40. This ballad is not in the De la Garza–Yturri Papers, private collection.

41. Affectionately called "General Polecat" by the Texans he commanded, Camille Armand Jules Marie, Prince de Polignac was the only noncitizen to achieve the rank of major general for either side during the Civil War. A French-born veteran of the Crimean War, Polignac was a lieutenant colonel on the staff of Gen. Pierre Gustave Toutant Beauregard. He was promoted to brigadier general, fought bravely at Shiloh and Corinth,

and transferred to the Trans-Mississippi Department in March 1863. At the Battle of Mansfield he commanded a brigade in Maj. Gen. Alfred Mouton's division and took command when Mouton was killed. After Pleasant Hill Polignac pursued Banks for more than a month. He was made major general, and in January 1865 was sent to France to lobby Napoleon III for favorable treatment of the Confederacy. After the Civil War he was decorated for bravery in the Franco-Prussian War and died in Paris on November 15, 1913, the last surviving Confederate major general. Legg, "Camille J. Polignac," 2:1,222–3; Warner, *Generals in Gray*, 242; Barr, *Polignac's Texas Brigade*, 21.

42. New York–born H. B. Adams was a captain and quartermaster in Col. Thomas N. Waul's Texas Legion. Taken prisoner at Vicksburg on July 4, 1863, Adams was paroled and then exchanged. He is listed on the 1860 Bexar County census as a twenty-six-year-old clerk with no personal property or real estate. Adams CSR; Eighth Census, 1860, Bexar County, Tex.; Hasskarl and Hasskarl, *Waul's Texas Legion*, 119. Adams wrote Bart DeWitt from Minden, Louisiana, on April 19, 1864, with details of the death of Captain de la Garza at the Battle of Mansfield. See letter dated April 19, 1864, below.

43. In 1863, during his siege of Port Hudson, Louisiana, Major General Banks was determined to clear all Confederate opposition west of the Mississippi River by pushing Federal forces up the Atchafalaya River and Bayou Teche. After the fall of Port Hudson on July 9, only days after the surrender of Vicksburg, the campaign into western Louisiana continued, with action around Alexandria.

44. Polignac's Texas Brigade consisted of the 22nd, 31st, and 34th Texas Cavalry as well as the 17th Texas Consolidated Cavalry (all dismounted) and the 15th Texas Infantry. Consistently plagued by morale and discipline problems, the brigade was, as historian Alwyn Barr has described, an "oddly assorted unit." Wooster, *Lone Star Regiments in Gray*, 247–62; Barr, *Polignac's Texas Brigade*, xv.

The Kentucky-born Almerine M. Alexander was a merchant who ran stores in several towns in northeastern Texas before the war. He raised the 34th Texas Cavalry in the winter of 1861–62 at Sherman, Texas. It was one of three Texas cavalry regiments brigaded for the first time in July 1862, fighting Federal troops at Spring River and Newtonia, Missouri, in the fall of 1862 and later at Prairie Grove, Arkansas in early December. Weakened by sickness, poor morale, and frequent desertions, the 34th was redesignated as an infantry unit and merged with the 15th Texas Infantry. In the autumn of 1863, Alexander returned home because of poor health and died in New Orleans in the summer of 1865. Cecil Harper Jr., "Almerine M. Alexander," *Handbook of Texas* Online, http://www.tshaonline.org/handbook/online/articles/AA/fa16.html (accessed Feb. 14, 2008).

James G. Stevens was elected major in the 22nd Texas Cavalry and eventually came to command the regiment as colonel. Citing his inability to control his men, Stevens resigned his commission in the autumn of 1863 and returned home to Hunt County, Texas. In 1867 he moved to Dallas, where he became superintendent of schools and vice president of the veterans of Polignac's Brigade. Stevens died there on May 24, 1889. Wooster, *Lone Star Regiments in Gray*, 248–49, 256, 326.

45. Evergreen was a small community five miles east of Bunkie, fifty miles north of Lafayette, and twenty-one miles west of the Mississippi River in south-central Louisiana.

46. M. Brown is probably María Brown, the daughter of María Josefa Refugio and Andrés Brown. Chabot, *Makers of San Antonio*, 170.

47. Green's Brigade was the old Sibley Brigade that had seen action at Valverde, Glorieta, and Peralta in New Mexico Territory in 1861–62. After Brig. Gen. Henry H. Sibley was called to Richmond to account for the New Mexico disaster, the brigade was led by Col. Tom Green and participated in the recapture of Galveston on January 1, 1863. Sibley resumed command of the brigade after it was transferred to Louisiana, but following the Confederate defeat at the Battle of Bisland on April 13–14, he was ordered before a court-martial by Maj. Gen. Richard Taylor and removed from command. In July Colonel Green led part of the brigade in an attack on the Federal garrison at Brashear City, Louisiana, before moving east to assault Donaldsonville on the Mississippi River. After returning to Texas in December 1863 to guard the coast near Galveston, the brigade was countermarched to Louisiana to join General Taylor in time to play a major role in the decisive actions of the Red River Campaign at Mansfield (April 6, 1864) and at Pleasant Hill (April 9). Promoted to brigadier general, Green soon after was killed at Blair's Landing on the Red River while leading an attack on a fleet of Union gunboats; Col. William Polk Hardeman assumed command of the brigade. After brief duty at Vidalia, on the Mississippi River opposite Natchez, the brigade was ordered to Arkansas in the fall of 1864. Most of the men were in Houston in May 1865 when they were surrendered as part of the Trans-Mississippi command. Hall, *Sibley's New Mexico Campaign;* Thompson, *Confederate General of the West;* Frazier, *Blood & Treasure.*

48. James Harrison rose to command the 15th Texas Infantry. Al-

though initially disappointed at not immediately being given a brigade to command, Harrison was later promoted to brigadier general. A businessman and Baptist layman from Waco, he became trustee of Baylor University but was paralyzed in 1873 and died in Waco on February 23, 1875. Wooster, *Lone Star Generals in Gray*, 135–37.

After the deaths of Benjamin F. Terry and Thomas Lubbock and the promotion of John A. Wharton, Thomas Harrison, James Harrison's younger brother, came to command Terry's Texas Rangers. Tom Harrison had fought with Jefferson Davis's Mississippi regiment during the Mexican War but afterward remained in Texas, where he practiced law in Houston and Marlin. Wounded three times and with five horses killed under him while commanding the rangers, Harrison was personally courageous but did not possess the polished and personal skills of his predecessors, being remembered by one of his men as small, nervous, and irascible. After the war he resumed the practice of law in Waco, became district judge, and a Democratic presidential elector in 1872. He died in Waco on July 14, 1891, and was buried beside his brother in the First Street Cemetery. Wooster, *Lone Star Regiments in Gray*, 48–50, 56, 253, 319.

49. Twisting and turning 250 miles through eastern Carroll, Madison, and Tensas parishes in northeastern Louisiana, the Tensas (or Tensaw) River unites with the Ouachita River southeast of Winnsboro to form the Black River.

50. This was probably due to smallpox, a highly contagious and often fatal disease in the nineteenth century. Symptoms include severe headache, high fever, general aches and pains, and possible delirium. Red, pus-filled blisters appeared on the body, and when the patient recovers, the pustules dry, form a scab, and leave a pitted scar. Smallpox could be prevented by vaccination then, but at the time of the Civil War, many people had not been vaccinated. The *San Antonio Semi-Weekly News* reported an outbreak in the city in May 1863. Cases of smallpox were "almost continually being brought here from the Rio Grande," the newspaper complained. *San Antonio Semi-Weekly News*, May 28, 1863; Schroeder-Lein, *Civil War Medicine*, 278–79.

51. W. A. Ryan was a major in the 17th Texas Dismounted Cavalry and became a lieutenant colonel when the 6th, 7th, and 10th Texas Infantry were consolidated with the 15th, 16th, 17th, 18th, 24th, and 25th Texas Dismounted Cavalry only weeks before the Confederate breakup in Texas. Ryan CSR.

52. Located half a mile north of the village of Harrisonburg in Cata-

houla Parish, Fort Beauregard was one of four Confederate forts guarding the Ouachita River. In 1863 the fort had been unsuccessfully attacked by four Union gunboats.

53.   María Antonia, eighteen, and Margarita, sixteen, were the daughters of José Antonio Navarro and Juana Chávez and the grandchildren of the famous José Antonio Navarro of Texas Revolution fame. María married John C. Ross, while Margarita married Robert Langston. Each couple became the parents of six children. Chabot, *Makers of San Antonio,* 205.

54.   This was Julius F. Wurzbach, twenty-four, who enlisted in Company H, 3rd Texas Infantry at San Antonio in September 1862.

55.   Tom Green was born in Mecklenburg County, Virginia, on June 9, 1814. After moving to Tennessee with his family, Green attended Princeton College and Jackson College, both in Tennessee, and took up the study of law. He arrived in Texas in 1835 and, as a private, helped man the famous "Twin Sisters" at the Battle of San Jacinto. Green later fought Comanches and served as a lieutenant colonel in the Army of the Republic of Texas. Active in the Mexican War, he was with Col. John Coffee Hays at the Battle of Monterrey. In command of the 5th Texas Mounted Volunteers in 1861, he fought bravely during Sibley's New Mexico Campaign, especially at the Battle of Valverde, and gallantly commanded the Sibley Brigade in Louisiana at Mansfield and Pleasant Hill on April 8 and 9. Green was killed in an attack on Federal gunboats on the Red River at Blair's Landing on April 12 when a shell from one vessel tore away a portion of his skull above the right eye. Faulk, *General Tom Green;* Faulk, "Confederate Hero at Val Verde," 300–11; Millett, "When General Green Was Killed," 408–9; Barr, "Tom Green"; Barr, "Battle of Blair's Landing," 204–12; Hall, *Confederate Army of New Mexico,* 133–34.

Born at Opelousas, Louisiana, on February 18, 1892, the son of a former governor and U.S. senator from Louisiana, Jean Jacques Alfred Alexander Mouton graduated from West Point in 1850. He resigned his commission shortly thereafter, however, to become a railroad construction engineer and brigadier general of Louisiana militia. At the beginning of the war, Mouton was elected colonel of the 18th Louisiana Infantry and fought bravely at Shiloh, where he was severely wounded. After recuperating, he was given command of a brigade and promoted to brigadier general. Commanding a division during the 1864 Red River Campaign, he was killed during a charge on the Union lines at Mansfield on April 8. Warner, *Generals in Gray,* 222–23; Legg, "Jean Jacques Alfred Alexander Mouton," 3:1092.

56.   After the fall of Vicksburg, Maj. Gen. Frederick Steele was placed

in command of the Federal army in Arkansas and ordered to clear the state of Rebel forces. After capturing Little Rock in September 1863, he was directed to cooperate with Banks's 1864 Red River Campaign in Louisiana but only got as far south as Camden, Arkansas. After learning that Banks had been defeated at Mansfield, Steele fell back to the Arkansas capital.

57.   Powhattan (or Powhatten) Bell, twenty-eight, was a private in Col. George M. Flournoy's 16th Texas Infantry. Surviving the war, he signed his parole papers at San Antonio on October 2, 1865. Bell is listed on the 1860 census as a Tennessee-born silversmith. Bell CSR; Eighth Census, 1860, Bexar County, Tex.

58.   Alice, twenty-two, and Annie, twenty, were the sociable daughters of George H. Sweet, editor of the *San Antonio Herald*, inspector general of militia, and a colonel in the Confederate Army. Eighth Census, 1860, Bexar County, Tex.; Marks, *When Will the Weary War Be Over*, 58, 73, 76, 97, 101–102, 113, 170, 191. See also n. 27.

59.   See n. 42.

PART 2. LETTERS OF CAPT. MANUEL YTURRI

1.   The Prussian-born Fritz Messinger was identified after the war as a thirty-six-year-old blacksmith. Ninth Census, 1870, Bexar County, Tex. A Scottish immigrant, James Duff settled in San Antonio, where he married and set up a mercantile business. Age thirty-three at the beginning of the war, he, his wife, and their two daughters lived in the city's Third Ward, where he claimed personal property of $26,000 and real estate of $9,000. Duff rose from captain to command the 33rd Texas Cavalry, or Duff's Partisan Rangers. He is perhaps best remembered today for his ruthless and brutal suppression and persecution of German Unionists in the Texas Hill Country. After the war Duff was indicted in Kendall County for his hanging of Unionists but fled to Denver, London, and then France, where he died. Eighth Census, 1860, Bexar County, Tex.; Duff Compiled Service Record, Confederate Adjutant General's Office, RG 109, NA (hereafter CSR); *San Antonio Daily Express*, Aug. 3, 1869.

2.   Son of the village tailor, James R. Sweet was born in Bridgetown, Nova Scotia, in 1818. As a young man, he eloped with Charlotte James and settled at St. John's, New Brunswick. After business failures, and at the suggestion of his brother-in-law, John James, Sweet moved to San Antonio in 1849 and entered the mercantile business. There he bought land at the head of the San Antonio River, near what is today Alamo Heights, and built a

large home; the property was later purchased by George W. Brackenridge and, later yet, became the site of Incarnate Word College. A leading member of the Know-Nothing Party, Sweet served as mayor of San Antonio from January 1, 1855, until January 1, 1856, and again from January 1, 1859, to May 26, 1862, when he resigned to enter the Confederate Army as a lieutenant. He rose rapidly to become lieutenant colonel of the 33rd Texas Cavalry. Sweet was active early in the war in the lower Rio Grande Valley, and Brig. Gen. Hamilton P. Bee put him in charge of purchasing cotton for the Confederacy in southeast Texas along the lower Brazos and Trinity rivers; Brig. Gen. Henry H. Sibley wrote that Sweet was of "high standing and integrity." He was paroled at Brownsville on October 6, 1865, and fearing Federal retribution, fled to Mexico with John B. Magruder, Joseph O. Shelby, and other Confederate officers and public officials. Sweet settled at the Confederate colony near Cordova, but in 1867 he returned to San Antonio and in 1873 bought an interest in the *San Antonio Daily Herald*. The 1880 census lists him as "paralized." Sweet died in the Alamo City a short time later, on December 12, 1880, and was buried in the City Cemetery. Pease, *They Came to San Antonio,* 232; S. W. Pease, "James R. Sweet," *Handbook of Texas* Online, http://www.tshaonline.org/handbook/online/articles/SS/fsw11.html (accessed Mar. 12, 2008); "Biographical Sketch, James Robert Sweet (1818–1880)," Sweet Family of New Brunswick, Canada, http://www3.nbnet.nb .ca/bobsweet/biograph.htm (accessed Mar. 12, 2008); Sweet CSR; and *San Antonio Express,* Dec. 13, 1880.

3. For Ignacio Cassiano, see part 1, n. 16. José García was a third lieutenant in Company H, 33rd Texas Cavalry (Duff's Partisan Rangers). Twenty-five years old at the time of his enlistment, he was promoted to first lieutenant and then placed in command of the company. After the war García became active in the Republican Party in Laredo. García CSR; Jerry Thompson, *Warm Weather and Bad Whiskey* (El Paso: Texas Western Press, 1991), 37–38. Severo Losoya, or "Learro Losoyo," as he is listed in Confederate records, enrolled in Duff's Partisan Rangers at San Antonio in May 1862. Twenty-nine years old, he was given a medical discharge for unknown reasons in November 1863. Losoya CSR.

4. Perhaps Yturri meant to write "D. P. R." for Duff's Partisan Rangers or "T. P. R." for Texas Partisan Rangers, instead of "T. P. D."

5. Born in Virginia in 1825, Philip Nolan Luckett went west to Ohio with his family at an early age. Although appointed to West Point, he failed to graduate and instead studied medicine and moved to Corpus Christi in 1847. In 1850 he served with John S. "Rip" Ford's Texas Rangers in South

Texas. Unmarried, he is listed in the 1860 census with real estate of $5,000 and personal property of $1,000. In 1861 Luckett was selected to represent Nueces and Webb counties at the Texas Secession Convention. Subsequently, in February 1861, he became part of the "Committee of Public Safety" that coerced and intimidated General Twiggs into surrendering the Department of Texas. Shortly thereafter, he was part of the hastily recruited Confederate army that forced the surrender of Federal forces at the Battle of Adams Hill near San Lucia Springs, some sixteen miles west of San Antonio. Despite his reputation as a heavy drinker, Luckett commanded the 3rd Texas Infantry at Brownsville, Galveston, and in Louisiana during the Red River Campaign. With the surrender of Confederate forces in the Trans-Mississippi, Luckett, sick and riding in an ambulance, set out for Mexico with four companions. He later returned to San Antonio only to be arrested and escorted to New Orleans under heavy guard. Indicted for high treason, he was held at Fort Jackson in a tiny casemate along with Sacfield Maclin, Dr. William McKendree Gwin, and Judge Thomas Jefferson Devine. Although he was released, Luckett's health was broken. Consequently, he traveled to Cincinnati, Ohio, to live with relatives and died there on May 21, 1869. Pease, *They Came to San Antonio*, 153–56; Eighth Census, 1860, Nueces County, Tex.; McPherson, "Plan of William McKendree Gwin," 357–86; Sacfield Maclin to G. T. Howard, Dec. 10, 1865, Howard Papers, Library of the Daughters of the Republic of Texas at the Alamo, San Antonio.

6. Richard T. Taylor commanded Company A of Duff's 33rd Texas Partisan Rangers, serving ably in the lower Rio Grande Valley early in the war. It was Taylor who observed the landing of Federal forces on Brazos Island on November 3, 1863. In May 1864, after obtaining a seventy-five-day leave of absence and assignment to court-martial duty in San Antonio, he announced as a candidate for county clerk of Bexar County. Consequently, Brig. Gen. Henry E. McCulloch accused him of "showing a disposition to avoid the service" and asked that he be ordered to return to his company at Brenham. Instead, Taylor resigned on October 26, 1864. Taylor CSR; R. Taylor to James Duff, Nov. 3, 1862, *War of the Rebellion*, ser. 1, 26(1):443–44; Thompson and Jones, *Civil War and Revolution on the Rio Grande Frontier*, 57; Thompson, *Vaqueros in Blue and Gray*, 76–77.

7. A *legua* is 5,572 meters.

8. Older brother of Brig. Gen. Barnard E. Bee, who was killed at the First Battle of Bull Run, Hamilton P. Bee rose to command Confederate forces on the Rio Grande frontier until the Federals chased him from Brownsville in November 1863. A large slaveowner, Bee was active in Loui-

siana during the 1864 Red River Campaign. After a poverty-plagued exile at Parras, Coahuila, he returned to Texas. Said to have been a heavy drinker, especially in the latter decades of his life, he died in San Antonio in 1897. Legg, "Hamilton P. Bee," 1:151; Meiners, "Bee in the Red River Campaign," 21–44.

9. A Mexican-born silversmith, Pedro Cevallos entered Confederate service in December 1861 and helped raised what became Company F, 3rd Texas Infantry. Although a senior captain in the regiment, he was forced to resign in November 1863, largely because he was "a Mexican and of limited English education." The resignation was said to have been "an act of charity to his family" because senior officers in the regiment did "not wish to disgrace him." In 1864, however, Cevallos became an ordnance officer in Col. Santos Benavides's regiment in the more relaxed ethnic environment at Laredo. After the war he became a deputy sheriff in Bexar County. Thompson, *Vaqueros in Blue and Gray*, 141; Cevallos CSR; Ninth (1870) and Tenth (1880) Censuses, Bexar County, Tex.

10. A thirty-eight-year-old attorney from San Antonio, Samuel Newton enlisted in the Confederate Army for "three years or the war" in March 1862 and rose to command Company H, 3rd Texas Infantry before becoming inspector general and lieutenant colonel. He was paroled at San Antonio on August 4, 1865, and afterward practiced law in the Alamo City. The 1860 Bexar County census enumerates Newton as having been born in Missouri, yet the 1870 census (presuming this is the same Samuel G. Newton), lists his birthplace as the Indian Territory. Newton CSR; Eighth (1860) and Ninth (1870) Censuses, Bexar County, Tex.

11. Upon entering Confederate service in the summer of 1861, Dominick Lively was assigned as acting adjutant at Camp Verde, in the Texas Hill Country, where Federal prisoners were confined. Although he was not re-elected as second lieutenant when Company A, 3rd Texas Infantry was reorganized in the late summer of 1862, he eventually became a captain in Company C of the regiment. At Fort Brown in April 1862, he was appointed acting adjutant on the staff of Col. John S. Ford. As a prisoner of war following the surrender at Arkansas Post in January 1863, he was exchanged and discharged from Gratiot Prison in St. Louis, Missouri, in April 1864. Lively CSR.

Señora French is probably Sarah L. French, the Michigan-born wife of James Henry French, who later served as mayor of San Antonio from January 1875 until January 1885. Born in Detroit, Michigan, Sarah came with her parents to Port Lavaca when she was only three. Settling in San

Antonio in 1846, she was said to have been "a great favorite in society, having a brilliant mind, while the prominence of her own and her husband's family gave her unusual opportunities to meet and know the leading Texans and visitors to the state before the war." Chabot, *Makers of San Antonio,* 319–20 (quote); Carolyn Hyman, "James Henry French," *Handbook of Texas* Online, http://www.tshaonline.org/handbook/online/articles/FF/ffr12.html (accessed Mar. 11, 2008).

12.   Camp Slaughter was located on the Brazos River near Columbia and was named for Brig. Gen. James E. Slaughter, who commanded the Western Subdistrict of Texas at the time. The post had a large hospital and several barracks. Winsor, *Texas in the Confederacy,* 33.

13.   The German-born Julius Hafner (Haffner), with whom Manuel Yturri threatened a duel on one occasion, was thirty-six at this time. He listed his occupation as "city collector" on the 1860 Bexar County census. Indeed, records indicate Hafner served as tax collector for the city from January 1, 1858, until January 1, 1861. His incomplete service record indicates that he first served in two companies of the 36th Texas Cavalry before being elected second lieutenant and then first lieutenant in Company F, 3rd Texas Infantry. Eighth Census, 1860, Bexar County, Tex.; Hafner CSR

14.   By the summer of 1863, the price of corn in San Antonio had risen to three dollars a bushel. *San Antonio Semi-Weekly News,* June 4, 1863.

15.   Lito (Manuelito), or Manuel, oldest child of Capt. Manuel Yturri and Elena de la Garza, was born on January 19, 1861, with a serious rupture, an ailment that plagued him as a child and well into his early adolescence. The well-known Texas painter Carl G. von Iwonski painted Manuel when he was only eight months of age. After marriage to Wina Hebgen, the couple remained childless. Manuel died on June 26, 1933. Chabot, *Makers of San Antonio,* 223; tombstone, St. Mary's Cemetery, San Antonio; John Yturri, interview with editor, Mar. 2, 2008. See also n. 24.

16.   This reference is to either Ernest or Victor, the first and second sons of Vicenta Yturri and Ernest B. Edmunds. A daughter, Ida, followed on May 1, 1865. Chabot, *Makers of San Antonio,* 223; "Sister Ida," tombstone inscription, Mission Burial Park No. 1, San Antonio, Tex.

17.   Born in Baltimore, Maryland, Elizabeth Ryman was the fifty-nine-year-old wife of Jacob Ryman, a stockraiser in Atascosa County. "Chepita" was the nickname for Joseph de la Garza's older sister, Josefina, who was married to John C. Crawford. Eighth (1860) and Ninth (1870) Censuses, Atascosa County, Tex. See also part 1, n. 19.

18.   From Atascosa County, twenty-five-year-old Allison Ryman was

a lieutenant in Company G, 3rd Texas Infantry. He was the center of an incident at Fort Brown in the early morning hours of December 6, 1862, when 100 men overwhelmed the guard and dragged a prisoner, who was accused of murdering two sergeants, out of the guardhouse and executed him. Rymer was paroled at San Antonio on September 15, 1865. He is listed on the 1870 census as a stockraiser living with his mother and father near Pleasanton. Ryman CSR; Ninth Census, 1870, Atascosa County, Tex. See also n. 17.

19.   Twenty-five-year-old Henry McCormack, five-feet, six-inches tall and born in Chetham, Ireland, enlisted in the 3rd Texas Infantry at Camp Verde on September 13, 1861. He became sergeant major before being promoted to first lieutenant and then regimental adjutant at Fort Brown in January 1863. Following the collapse of the Confederacy in the Trans-Mississippi, he signed his parole papers at San Antonio on August 28, 1865. McCormack CSR.

20.   "El frijol" in the original letter probably refers to the coral.

21.   The San Bernard River rises one mile south of New Ulm, in southwestern Austin County, and flows southeast for 120 miles before entering the Gulf of Mexico a few miles down the coast from Freeport.

22.   Yturri's second child, Elena, was named after her mother. Chabot, *Makers of San Antonio*, 223.

23.   Mary Hafner was the twenty-three-year-old wife of Julius Hafner, San Antonio tax collector, who became a lieutenant in the 3rd Texas Infantry. The couple is listed on the 1860 census with one child, Pauline, age five. Eighth Census, 1860, Bexar County, Tex. See also n. 13.

24.   Crail may be the father of Charles N. Crail, an Italian-born San Antonio merchant. Solya is probably Juan Anselmo Losoya, a leading citizen of San Antonio, after whom Losoya Street is named. A. Eule served as assessor for the City of San Antonio in 1863. His widow, Prussian-born Ammie, fifty-two, and their three children are listed on the 1870 Bexar County census. Ninth Census, 1870, Bexar County, Tex.

The "painter" is probably Prussian-born Carl G. von Iwonski, bachelor artist who came to New Braunfels in 1845 and moved to San Antoni, in the late 1850s. On the eve of the war, Iwonski painted Manuel Yturri in hunting gear, along with his dog Guess, probably on the banks of the San Antonio River. After the war began, Iwonski made sketches of Texas state troops in San Antonio and at Las Moras Creek near Fort Clark; the latter was the first Civil War sketch reproduced in *Harper's Weekly*. Iwonski's dramatic painting of Terry's Texas Rangers galloping off to war is one of the more famous Texas Civil War images. During Reconstruction, he became a Radical Republican and, with colleague Hermann Lungkwitz, set up a photographic studio in San Antonio while continuing as a portrait painter. Iwonski served as city tax collector but was removed from office in May 1870. He returned with his mother to Germany in 1873 and died there on April 4, 1912. More than one hundred of his Texas images have been identified. McGuire, *Iwonski in Texas,* 33, 42–44; James Patrick McGuire, "Carl G. von Iwonski," in *New Handbook of Texas,* 3:882; Pinckney, *Painting in Texas.*

25.   In a bend of the Navasota River, the community of Navasota was served by several stage lines and, after 1859, the Houston and Texas Central Railroad. The community became an important shipping and marketing center during the Civil War, when considerable cotton, gunpowder, and guns were stored in various buildings there. At the end of the war, disgruntled Confederate soldiers torched one warehouse filled with cotton and gunpowder; the blast from the resulting explosion killed several citizens and started a fire that destroyed several other buildings, including the post office. John Leffler, "Navasota, Texas," *Handbook of Texas* Online, http://tshaonline .org/handbook/online/articles/NN/hfn1.html (accessed Dec. 23, 2007).

26.   Born at Wurtemberg, Germany, on May 14, 1825, John R. Rosenheimer came to San Antonio in 1848, worked as a clerk for Louis Zork, and married Dolores Concepción Barrera. Claiming to have been "one of the original Secessionists" and a proud member of the Knights of the Golden Circle, Rosenheimer ran for state representative from Bexar County in 1861 and was defeated, but soon afterward he was appointed first lieutenant of Company F, 3rd Texas Infantry on December 13, 1861. During the Civil War, he commanded the company at Fort Brown in the spring of 1862 before being appointed provost marshal. When Capt. Pedro Cevallos resigned in November 1863, Rosenheimer was made captain. Said to be myopic and obese, with a case of hemorrhoids so severe, he asserted in June 1863, that he was losing "great quantities of blood," he was declared unfit for duty at Monroe, Louisiana, in September 1864 and given a medical discharge. After the war he served as city secretary in 1865, Bexar County judge from July 1866 until August 1868, and city secretary again from 1877 to 1879. After the amputation of one of his arms, Rosenheimer died on August 26, 1885, and was buried in the Odd Fellows Cemetery in San Antonio. Rosenheimer CSR; Pease, *They Came to San Antonio,* 212; *San Antonio Semi-Weekly News,* Nov. 7, 1861.

27.   This is probably Florina, New York–born wife of John Binns, an

Irish immigrant who settled in San Antonio. Eighth Census, 1860, Bexar County, Tex.

28. Tata is Mariano Rodríguez, a wealthy Bexareño who organized the San Fernando Rangers for the Mexican government in the months prior to March 1836. Because of this Don Mariano, as he was affectionately known to family and friends, was forced to flee San Antonio following Santa Anna's defeat at San Jacinto. After living in Mexico for twelve years, he returned to San Antonio following the Treaty of Guadalupe-Hidalgo in 1848. In the years that followed, Rodríguez struggled to regain his lands and a measure of his former wealth. John Yturri, interview with editor, Feb. 24, 2008; Rodríguez, *Memoirs of Early Texas,* 52–54.

29. Simeon Hart, a New York–born civil engineer, came to the Southwest as an adjutant in the Missouri cavalry during the Mexican War. In 1849, along with his wife, Jesusita Siqueiros, the daughter of a wealthy Chihuahua flour miller, Hart settled at what is today El Paso, where he built a flourmill, El Molino, and obtained several contracts to supply the army with flour. In 1860, with real and personal property valued at $350,000, he was by far the wealthiest man in the area. But much of his wealth was lost during the Civil War after he cast his lot with the Confederacy. W. H. Timmons, "Simeon Hart," *New Handbook of Texas,* 3:492; Smith, *U.S. Army and the Texas Frontier Economy,* 83, 107, 260.

30. Theodore E. Giraud was the brother of the famed San Antonio architect François Giraud and probably born at Charleston, South Carolina. In 1847 he came to San Antonio with his father, who was the French consul. Sometime prior to the war, Theodore settled in Houston with his wife, Catherine. Pease, *They Came to San Antonio,* 113.

31. The only C. C. Clute listed on the 1860 census was a resident of Schenectady, New York. The "express agent" may have been a relative of James E. Clute, who was living at Houston in 1860, and enlisted in Hood's Texas Brigade, only to be killed at Cold Harbor, Virginia, on June 17, 1862, during the Peninsula Campaign.

32. Douglas is near Hope Pond, Texas, eleven miles east of Tyler in eastern Smith County.

33. George Cupples, a pioneer surgeon and civic leader in San Antonio, was thought to be the first physician in Texas to use surgical anesthetics. Born in Scotland, he graduated in medicine at the University of Edinburgh in 1838 and afterward studied at the University of Paris. On the advice of Dr. Ashbel Smith, Cupples moved to Texas in 1844 and settled in San Antonio as a member of Henri Castro's colony. He was elected president of the Bexar

County Medical Society, served as city health physician, and became the first president of the Texas Medical Association. Cupples is listed with real estate of $4,000 and personal property valued at $4,000 on the 1860 census. He was a surgeon in the Mexican War under Col. Jack Hays, and in the Civil War he held the same position with the 7th Regiment of Texas Mounted Volunteers in Sibley's Army of New Mexico. In December 1862 he became medical director of the Eastern Military District of Texas and in June 1864 was appointed medical director in the Trans-Mississippi Department. After the war Cupples returned to San Antonio and continued his medical practice. He died at his home in San Antonio on April 19, 1895. Green, *Place Names of San Antonio,* 39; Robert Read Nixon, "George Cupples," *Handbook of Texas* Online, http://www.tshaonline.org/handbook/online/articles/CC/fcu25.html (accessed Dec. 24, 2007); Hall, *Confederate Army of New Mexico,* 222; Eighth (1860) and Tenth (1880) censuses, Bexar County, Tex.; *San Antonio Daily Herald,* Feb. 20, 1867.

34. This may have been William Preston Payne of Company C, 37th Texas Cavalry.

35. Although at least seven individuals with the name of Campbell, most of them stockmen, were residents of Bexar County at the time, this individual is likely Martin Campbell, a prominent Louisiana-born resident of San Antonio who served as city alderman in 1860 and again in 1865–66. Eighth Census, 1860, Bexar County, Tex.

36. Bavarian-born gunsmith Jacobo Lynn (Linn), twenty-one, is enumerated on the 1860 San Antonio census with real estate of $12,000 and personal property of $20,000. With his shop on Military Plaza, Lynn advertised in the *San Antonio Semi-Weekly News* from January 1862 until July 1863, offering to sell "hand guns and pistols." Eighth Census, 1860, Bexar County, Tex.; *San Antonio Semi-Weekly News,* Feb. 1862, July 7, 1863.

37. Elena, or Leontine as she was known to the family, was the oldest daughter of Manuel and Elena Yturri. She married Wilhelm Marx, and the couple came to parent five children, Fritz, Elena, Victor, Howard, and Edwin. Chabot, *Makers of San Antonio,* 223. For her older brother, Manuel (or Lito), see n. 15.

38. Originally from Sabinas Hidalgo, Nuevo León, Meliton Hernández was eighteen years old and five feet, six inches in height. He first enrolled in Capt. F. J. Parker's Company C, 3rd Texas Infantry at Brownsville in October 1861. After serving at Ringgold Barracks and transferring to Company F, he deserted at Fort Brown on April 29, 1862. Hernandez CSR.

Marcos Garza enrolled as a private in Company F, 33rd Texas Infantry. His compiled service record is incomplete, and there is no indication of his desertion. Garza CSR.

Andrés Gonzalez was twenty-five years old; five feet, five inches in height; and a native of Matamoros, Tamaulipas, when he enrolled as a private in Company C, 3rd Texas Infantry at Fort Brown in October 1861, receiving a fifty-dollar bounty. He deserted while stationed at Brownsville on February 17, 1862, but was apprehended at Edinburg four months later. Ordered before a court-martial and found guilty of desertion, Gonzalez was sentenced to "hard labor" for the remainder of the war, to be dishonorably discharged, and to "wear an eighteen pound ball and chain attached to his leg." His pay was stopped except for one dollar a month for the prison laundress. Gonzalez CSR.

Eduardo Postel is certain to be Eduardo Postillo, a twenty-seven-year-old, five-foot-seven-inch-tall native of Zacatecas, Mexico, who enlisted in James N. Morgan's Company of the 3rd Texas Infantry. His service records do not indicate that he deserted. Postillo CSR.

39. During Maj. Gen. Nathaniel Banks's retreat down Red River in early May 1864, he assigned the 113th New York Infantry to protect Alexandria, where many Unionists were known to live. Despite Banks's orders, numerous buildings were burned and the town plundered; twenty-two blocks were said to have been consumed in the conflagration. Adm. David D. Porter, who had yet to depart downriver with his fleet, remarked that "the burning of Alexandria was a fit termination of the unfortunate Red River expedition." Porter, *Incidents and Anecdotes*, 258–59; Winters, *Civil War in Louisiana*, 372–75.

40. Early in the war, the Confederates began construction on nine forts that were arranged in a semicircle around Camden. After seizing Little Rock, in March 1864 Maj. Gen. Frederick Steele pushed his 14,000-man army toward Shreveport. Confederate major general Sterling Price worked diligently to fortify the city but in the face of the Federal advance, evacuated Camden, which Steele occupied on April 15, 1864. Two days later Steele sent 1,000 men, including 438 men of the 1st Kansas Colored Volunteers, with approximately 200 wagons to retrieve a large quantity of corn near Poison Springs, west of Camden. Two miles west of Poison Springs, Confederates blocked the route back to town, and in the fighting that followed, they completely routed the Union troops, capturing all the supply wagons. The Federals lost 301 men killed, wounded, or missing, while the Confederates suffered the loss of 114 men. After receiving the news that General Banks had been defeated at the Battle of Mansfield, Steele evacuated Camden on

April 26, and the Confederates again took possession of the city. Bailey, "Massacre at Poison Spring," 157–68.

41.   Born at Gallatin, Tennessee, on February 10, 1821, William R. Scurry moved to Texas in the late 1830s and settled at San Augustine. Before the age of twenty-one, he was licensed to practice law. Scurry fought in the Mexican War and practiced law in Austin, where he purchased an interest in the *Texas State Gazette* and served as coeditor of the newspaper. After selling his share in the newspaper, he moved to Victoria, where he was appointed a commissioner for the state of Texas to help survey the Texas–New Mexico boundary line along the thirty-second parallel. He later moved to Clinton, in De Witt County, where he was elected a delegate to the Secessionist Convention. Following secession, Scurry was appointed colonel of the 4th Texas Mounted Volunteers, led them during Sibley's 1861–62 New Mexico Campaign, commanded Confederate forces at the Battle of Glorieta, and was promoted to brigadier general in September 1862. He played a leading role in the recapture of Galveston on January 1, 1863, and was assigned to command the Third Brigade of Walker's Texas Division. After leading his brigade at Mansfield and Pleasant Hill in April 1864, Scurry was sent to Arkansas to help repel Frederick Steele's advance, meeting his fate on April 30 at the Battle of Jenkins' Ferry. He was buried in the Texas State Cemetery in Austin. Today Scurry County, at the foot of the Llano Estacado, honors his memory. Scurry CSR; Brown, *Journey to Pleasant Hill,* 355; Thomas J. Cutrer, "William Read Scurry," *New Handbook of Texas,* 5:946; Anderson, *Confederate General William R. "Dirty Neck Bill" Scurry;* Hall, *Confederate Army of New Mexico,* 54.

42.   Although General Steele was able to seize Camden in April 1864, he learned that Major General Price and Gen. E. Kirby Smith had join forces to drive him out. Moreover, Brig. Gen. James F. Fagan had destroyed a Union wagon train on its way from Camden toward Pine Bluff. Retreating from Camden, Steele pushed through rain and mud and deployed 4,000 men to cover his retreat across the Saline River. The Battle of Jenkins' Ferry on April 30 represented the final repulse of the Union Army during the Camden Expedition and cleared the way for a last Confederate raid of Missouri.

43.   A native of McNairy County, Tennessee, Horace Randal moved with his family to the vicinity of San Augustine, Texas, in 1839. Graduating from West Point in 1854, he served on the Texas frontier and in New Mexico Territory before resigning in February 1861. As colonel of the 28th Texas Cavalry, he was commended for his bravery at Milliken's Bend, during the Vicksburg Campaign, and at Mansfield and Pleasant Hill, during the Red

River Campaign. Commissioned a brigadier general, he was killed while leading his brigade at the Battle of Jenkins' Ferry on April 30, 1864, before receiving word of the promotion. Stephenson, "Horace Randal," 3:1305.

44.   Born in South Carolina on January 5, 1813, Thomas Waul studied at South Carolina College before becoming an attorney in Mississippi and migrating to Texas, where he became a slaveowner and planter near Gonzalez. In 1861 Waul was selected as one of seven representatives from Texas to the Confederate convention in Montgomery, Alabama. He proposed several bills that failed to pass, including one that would allow the importation of slaves from other parts of the Americas. Defeated in the race for the Confederate Senate, he began raising troops for what would become Waul's Legion. Composed of cavalry, infantry, and artillery, Waul's Legion was in the forefront of the fighting to secure Vicksburg before retreating into the defenses of the city and eventually surrendering on July 4, 1863. Exchanged and promoted to brigadier general in September 1863, Waul commanded an infantry brigade in Maj. Gen. John G. Walker's Texas Division during the 1864 Red River Campaign. After the battles of Mansfield and Pleasant Hill, General Kirby Smith sent Walker's Division north to assist General Price in halting the Union advance in Arkansas. At Jenkins' Ferry on April 30, Waul led a charge of his brigade that helped drive Frederick Steele back across the Saline River. Wounded in the arm, as Yturri mentions, he was given a furlough and returned to his home in Texas. After the war Waul became a leading attorney at Galveston but retired to a farm in rural Hunt County near Greenville in northern Texas. He died there on July 24, 1903. Barr, "Thomas N. Waul," 4:1695–96; Wooster, *Lone Star Regiments in Gray,* 100–106, 238–44, 327–28.

45.   Federal casualties at Jenkins' Ferry were placed at 528. Confederate casualties were close to 1,000 men, of whom 341 were from Walker's Texas Division; Waul's Brigade suffered 100 casualties in the fighting. Barr, "Texan Losses in the Red River Campaign," 103–10.

46.   Otto Amelung, thirty-one, enlisted in the 3rd Texas Infantry at San Antonio on March 15, 1862, and eventually served in F and H companies. Amelung CSR. Mrs. Giraud is probably Catherine Giraud, wife of Theodore Giraud, born in Charleston, South Carolina, to François and Adele Giraud. François Giraud, an architect, settled at San Antonio about 1847 and served as mayor of the city from November 1872 until January 1875. Among his architectural projects were the original buildings of St. Mary's College along the river and Ursuline Academy. Chabot, *Makers of San Antonio,* 264; Ninth Census, 1870, Bexar County, Tex.

47.   According to Mary Adams Maverick, wife of the influential Samuel Maverick, a flood swept through San Antonio on the evening of June 7, 1864. The San Antonio River rose twelve to fifteen feet, sweeping away homes and inundating others. The flood caused a number of adobe houses on the banks of the river to "crumble partly down." Although several citizens had to be rescued from the raging waters, only "one negro woman" was known to have drowned. Marks, *When Will the Weary War Be Over*, 152.

48.   The Black River is formed by the confluence of the Ouachita and Tensas rivers in east central Louisiana and runs 101 miles south to join the Red River. The Trinity River, rising in three principal branches just northwest of present-day Dallas, flows 550 miles into Trinity Bay, the northern portion of Galveston Bay, at Anahuac.

49.   A laborer born at Puebla, Mexico, José Belásquez [Velásquez] was five feet, four inches in height at the time he enlisted in Capt. F. J. Parker's Company C, 3rd Texas Infantry at Fort Brown on October 8, 1861. Velasques claimed his age was forty at the time he enlisted but later admitted to being sixty. He was subsequently discharged for "old age and debility that incapacitates him" at Alexandria, Louisiana, on July 18, 1864. Belasquez CSR.

Teodoro Zepeda, forty-five, enrolled in Capt. Pedro Cevallos's Company F, 3rd Texas Infantry at San Antonio on December 13, 1861. He is listed on the 1870 census in Atascosa County as single and a farm laborer living near Pleasanton. Zepeda CSR; Ninth Census, 1870, Atascosa County, Tex.

50.   Captain Yturri's father married María Josefa Isabel Rodríguez on August 20, 1821. Captain Yturri's maternal grandmother was María de Jesus Carvajal, the wife of Mariano Rodríguez, a captain in the Spanish and Mexican armies. Chabot, *Makers of San Antonio*, 74, 223.

51.   Robert Franklin does not appear on the 1860, 1870, or 1880 Texas censuses nor in Texas genealogical studies or family databanks or records.

52.   Timmy was a nickname for Leontine.

53.   Age twenty-three at the time of the war, Phil Shardein, whose name is spelled variously as "Shardine," "Shardein," "Schardein," and "Shardian" in Confederate records, rose to command Company G, 3rd Texas Infantry in June 1863. He signed his parole papers at San Antonio on August 28, 1865.

54.   Guess is probably the hunting dog depicted in Iwonski's painting of Manuel Yturri. See also n. 24.

55.   Martiniano Rodríguez was a private in Capt. Pedro Cevallos's Company F, 3rd Texas Infantry. Rodríguez CSR.

56.   The condemned was Capt. John Guynes, who commanded Com-

pany F, 22nd Texas Infantry. A farmer from Polk County, Guynes was found guilty of persuading and advising soldiers to desert by a court-martial at the division headquarters of Maj. Gen. John H. Forney. A Mexican War veteran from Big Sandy, he had enrolled in the Jeff Davis Guards at Livingston on March 10, 1862, elected a lieutenant, and paid a bounty of $100. Although sentenced to be "shot to death by musketry," the court recommended mercy since Guynes "was over conscript age" and of "good character." The "crime of desertion is so frequent, so heinous and so destructive to the best interest of our cause that officers who do not use their efforts to prevent it," Adj. Gen. Edmund P. Turner responded, "deserve to die ignomin[i]ously." Guynes's execution order was read twice before each regiment, and at 4:00 P.M. on the afternoon of October 15, Parson's, Churchill's, Polignac's, and Forney's infantry divisions were formed in a large field upriver from Camden to witness the execution. "The officer in command gave the order Ready— Aim—Fire—and he was no more," Pvt. Isaac Dunbar Affleck recalled, "he fell a corps[e], with six bullets through him. The crowd rushed up to him to look at him. I had seen enough and turned away from the sad and horrid sight." Another soldier wrote that Guynes was "an old man, above the conscript age, his hair tinged with gray." To yet another soldier, Guynes was "a man of about fifty years old, and very much admired by his men, and well liked by the officers of his brigade." In reality Guynes was thirty-nine. GO No. 58, District of Arkansas, Oct. 14, 1864, in Guynes CSR (first quote); Wooster, "With the Confederate Cavalry in the West," 20 (second quote); Lowe, *Walker's Texas Division*, 245 (third quote); Blessington, *Campaigns of Walker's Texas Division*, 279–80 (fourth quote).

57. The twenty-eight-year-old, footloose, Cuban-born Enrique D'Hamel enlisted for one year in Capt. Bethel Coopwood's San Elizario Spy Company at El Paso in April 1861; the company was attached to Col. John R. Baylor's 2nd Texas Mounted Rifles. In the fighting in New Mexico, D'Hamel was wounded in a skirmish with a detachment of New Mexico volunteers, receiving "a spent Springfield rifle bullet in my left wrist, which went up my arm almost to the elbow." At the conclusion of the New Mexico Campaign, D'Hamel volunteered to accompany a party of wealthy New Mexico Confederate sympathizers to Chihuahua; this group probably included former governor Manuel Armijo. In November 1862 he enlisted in Company G , 33rd Texas Cavalry and was appointed provost marshal for San Antonio. When he attempted to arrest three privates in the 33rd Cavalry, however, thirty-six men submitted what the lieutenant called a "mutinous & seditious" petition asserting that he was "wholly unfit and totally incom-

petent" for duty and called on him to resign. In response D'Hamel claimed that the company commander, Capt. J. B. Weyman, had instigated the petition. He also solicited a letter from Brig. Gen. Smith P. Bankhead saying that he was "an intelligent and efficient officer." Complaining of his "wounded arm," from which the bullet had never been removed, and also wanting to visit his aging parents in Havana, Cuba, D'Hamel resigned on September 17, 1864. He submitted several surgeon certificates from physicians at the San Antonio General Hospital that he was in great pain, in feeble health, and had also been wounded in the thighs and chest as well as suffering from "habitual prolapsus of the rectum." His resignation was accepted on October 26. In 1914 D'Hamel published his *Adventures of a Tenderfoot*. D'Hamel CSR; D'Hamel *Adventures of a Tenderfoot*, 12.

58. The "Painter" may well have been the noted Prussian artist Carl G. von Iwonski, who was living in San Antonio at the time and who sketched Texas troops in San Antonio and at Las Moras near Bracketville. See n. 24.

59. Richard Daly, a native of Uvalde County, rose from second lieutenant to captain in command of Company C, 3rd Texas Infantry. He was paroled by Union forces at San Antonio on September 29, 1865. Daly CSR.

60. Camp Sumter was located at Spring Hill, Hempstead County, Arkansas.

61. Weneceslao Ximenes (Jimenez) enrolled in Capt. Pedro Cevallos's Company F, 3rd Texas Infantry at San Antonio in April 1862 and was paid a bounty of fifty dollars. In November 1863 he was promoted to corporal. Ximenes CSR.

62. Sixteen miles south of Shreveport and eleven miles northwest of Mansfield, Keachi is a small community in De Soto Parish in northwestern Louisiana, near the Texas-Louisiana boundary.

63. Mary Picque, age fifty, is listed on the 1870 Natchitoche census with real estate of $500 and personal property of $125. At the time, she was living with her daughter, Annette Picque. Carlos Vital Picque served in the 2nd Louisiana Infantry as a private. Ninth Census, 1870, Natchitoches Parish, La.

64. Piedmont Springs was a popular resort and health spa in Grimes County. With three sulfur springs and a four-story, 100-room hotel, billiards, poker, numerous bathhouses, and a large bar, the springs were the social center for the area. Late in the war the hotel was converted to a hospital and the headquarters for Walker's Texas Division. "Piedmont Springs," *Handbook of Texas* Online, http://www.tshaonline.org/handbook/online/articles/PP/rpp8.html (accessed Dec. 24, 2007).

65.   Fifty miles northwest of Houston, Hempstead was the county seat of Waller County. The Houston and Texas Central Railroad had reached the community in 1858, helping make it a distribution center between the Gulf Coast and the interior of the state. During the Civil War, Hempstead served as a Confederate manufacturing center, and at least three camps were located in the vicinity. Carole E. Christian, "Hempstead, Texas," *Handbook of Texas* Online, http://www.tshaonline.org/handbook/online/articles/HH/hgh7.html (accessed Dec. 26, 2007); Spindler, "History of Hempstead."

66.   Named for the flamboyant Maj. Gen. John "Prince John" Magruder, Camp Magruder was located on the road from Shreveport, Louisiana, to Camden, Arkansas, amid a pine forest on a ridge just outside Menden, Louisiana. As many as 10,000 to 15,000 Confederates, many of them from Walker's Texas Division, were housed there during the winter of 1864–65. Many of the soldiers, as Captain Yturri earlier indicates, were housed in crude, hastily constructed log cabins. While at Camp Magruder, several men in Walker's Division deserted, were apprehended, sent before a court-martial, and when found guilty, taken to the Reagan Plantation, north of Menden, where they were executed and buried on site. Cutrer and Parrish, *Brothers in Gray*, 247; Agan, *Menden*, 36–40.

67.   Head of navigation on the Trinity River and near the site of a Spanish settlement called Atascosito, Liberty was the county seat of Liberty County and a major terminus of the Texas and New Orleans Railroad. With warehouses, trading posts, gristmills, two sawmills, and cattle-shipping docks as well as a ferry across the Trinity River, the community was also the trading center for surrounding plantations. Diana J. Kleiner, "Liberty, Texas," *Handbook of Texas* Online, http://www.tshaonline.org/handbook/online/articles/LL/hf14.html (accessed Feb. 13, 2008).

68.   Ten miles northeast of Navasota, Anderson was the county seat of Grimes County. Featuring two steam sawmills, cotton gins, the popular Fanthorp Inn, a hardware store, blacksmith shops, and a pistol factory that provided handguns for the Confederacy, Anderson was at one time during the war the fourth-largest community in Texas. Jan M. Hennigar, "Anderson, Texas," *Handbook of Texas* Online, http://www.tsha.utexas.edu/handbook/online/articles/AA/hla16.html (accessed Dec. 26, 2007).

69.   Veusilado Ximenes (Jimenes or Jimenez) was a private in Company F, 3rd Texas Infantry. He deserted at Ringgold Barracks on November 8, 1862, but was apprehended on December 10 and ordered to rejoin his company. Ximenes CSR.

70.   Sixteen miles southeast of Bryan in southern Brazos County, Milli-

can featured a post office, stagecoach station, and a terminus of the Houston and Texas Central Railway. At one time during the Civil War, Millican was the training camp for as many as 5,000 Confederate soldiers. Christina L. Gray, "Millican, Texas," *Handbook of Texas* Online, http://www.tsha.utexas.edu/handbook/online/articles/MM/hlm71.html (accessed Dec. 27, 2007).

71.　José Arizpe cannot be identified with certainty.

72.　Cresencio Navarro, age twenty-two, was a private in Capt. John M. Carolan's Company H of Woods Texas Cavalry of the 36th Texas Cavalry. Navarro CSR; Thompson, *Vaqueros in Blue and Gray,* 170.

73.　By his references to Lt. Julius Hafner, this letter appears to have been written sometime in late 1863.

74.　Nineteen when he mustered into the 3rd Texas Infantry, Leandro Bernal rose from fourth corporal to first sergeant of Company F. Bernal CSR; Thompson, *Vaqueros in Blue and Gray,* 136.

75.　In 1860 the English-born Tomas Whitehead, age fifty, was a stonemason living in the First Ward in San Antonio. He claimed $2,600 in personal property. Eighth Census, 1860, Bexar County, Tex.

76.　The Ohio-born E. C. Dewey is listed on the 1860 census as a farmer with real estate of $6,500 and personal property valued at $3,000. Eighth Census, 1860, Bexar County, Tex.

77.　This letter begins with the parenthetical number three at the top, obviously indicating the third page of a letter that was likely written sometime in 1864.

Bibliography

MANUSCRIPTS AND ARCHIVAL COLLECTIONS

Baptismal Records. Catholic Archives of San Antonio. San Antonio, Tex.

Bustillo Family Papers, 1772–1936. Daughters of the Republic of Texas Library at the Alamo, San Antonio.

Compiled Service Records of Volunteer Confederate Soldiers Who Served in Organizations from the State of Texas. Confederate Adjutant General's Office. Record Group 109. National Archives, Washington, D.C.

Adams, H. B.
Amelung, Otto
Bell, Powhatten
Bernal, Leandro
Bustillos, Antonio
Cassiano, Ignacio
Cevallos, Pedro
Costa, Joseph A.
Daly, Richard C.
De la Garza, Joseph Rafael
D'Hamel, Enrique Belleau
Duff, James A.
Finlay, George P.
Garza, Marcos
Gonzalez, Andres
Guynes, John
Hafner, Julius
Harvey, Robert B.
Hernandez, Meliton
Jimenez, Veusilado
Jimenez, Weneceslao
Lively, Dominick
Luckett, Philip Nolan
Martinez, Vicente
McCormack, Henry
McCowan, John J.

Navarro, Ángel
Navarro, Cresencio
Navarro, Eugenio
Navarro, José Ángel
Navarro, José Antonio
Navarro, Sixto Eusebio
Newton, Samuel G.
Placera, Simon Garza
Postel, Eduardo
Rodríguez, Martiniano
Rosenheimer, John R.
Ryan, W. A.
Ryman, Allison
Sandoval, Carlos
Scurry, William Read
Sharedin, Phil P.
Sweet, George H.
Sweet, James Robert
Taylor, Richard T.
Velasquez, José María
Wurzbach, Julius F.
Yturri, Manuel
Zarate, Pedro Ville
Zepeda, Teodoro
Zuniga, Antonio

Correspondencia de Santiago Vidaurri. Archivo General del Estado de Nuevo León, Monterrey, Mexico.

De la Garza Papers. Daughters of the Republic of Texas Library at the Alamo, San Antonio.

Eighth Census (1860). National Archives, Washington, D.C.
    Atascosa County, Tex.
    Bexar County, Tex.
    Caddo Parish, La.
    El Paso County, Tex.
    Harris County, Tex.
    Wilson County, Tex.

Howard, G. T., Papers. Library of the Daughters of the Republic of Texas at the Alamo, San Antonio.

Letters Received. Confederate Adjutant General's Office. Record Group 109. National Archives, Washington, D.C.

Letters Received. Department of Texas and the District of Texas, New Mexico, and Arizona. Record Group 365. National Archives, Washington, D.C.

Letters Received. Trans-Mississippi Department. Records of the Confederate War Department. Record Group 109. National Archives, Washington, D.C.

Marriage Records. County Clerk's Office, Bexar County, Tex.

Ninth Census, 1870. National Archives, Washington, D.C.
    Atascosa County, Tex.
    Bexar County, Tex.
    Natchitoches Parish, La.

Regimental Returns. 6th Texas Infantry. Confederate Adjutant General's Office. Record Group 109. National Archives, Washington, D.C.

Slave Census Schedules, 1850 and 1860. Record Group 29. National Archives, Washington, D.C.
    Bexar County, Tex.

Tenth Census, 1880. National Archives, Washington, D.C.
    Bexar County, Tex.
    Atascosa County, Tex.

Tombstone Inscriptions. San Antonio, Tex.
    Mission Burial Park No. 1
    St. Mary's Cemetery
    San Fernando No. 1 Cemetery

Twelfth Census, 1900. National Archives, Washington, D.C.
    Bexar County, Tex.

INTERVIEWS

DeWitt, Joe. Interview by Jerry Thompson, January 2, 2008.
Yturri, Helen. Interviews by Jerry Thompson, June 14, 1975; February 12,
    March 6, September 26, 2007; March 2, 2008.
Yturri, John. Interview by Jerry Thompson, March 2, 2008.

NEWSPAPERS

Austin: *Southern Intelligencer, State Gazette, Tri-Weekly State Gazette*
Brownsville: *American Flag, Ranchero*
Corpus Christi: *Ranchero*
Galveston: *News*
Houston: *Daily Telegraph*
New Orleans: *Picayune*
San Antonio: *Alamo Express, Alamo Star, Bejareño, Correo, Daily Express,
    Daily Herald, Daily Ledger, Light, Daily Texan, Ranchero, Semi-Weekly
    News, Sentinel, Western Texan*

BOOKS

Agan, John A. *Menden: Remembrance and Pride.* Mount Pleasant, S.C.:
    Arcadia, 2002.
Almaráz, Félix D., Jr. *The San Antonio Missions and Their System of Land
    Tenure.* Austin: University of Texas Press, 1989.
Anderson, Charles G. *Confederate General William R. "Dirty Neck Bill"
    Scurry, 1821–1864.* Tallahassee: Rose Printing, 1999.
Bailey, Ann J. *Between the Enemy and Texas.* Fort Worth: Texas Christian
    University Press, 1989.
Barr, Alwyn. *Polignac's Texas Brigade.* 1964. Reprint, College Station: Texas
    A&M University Press, 1998.
Baum, Dale. *The Shattering of Texas Unionism: Politics in the Lone Star
    State during the Civil War Era.* Baton Rouge: Louisiana State Univer-
    sity Press, 1998.
Blessington, Joseph Palmer. *The Campaigns of Walker's Texas Division.*
    Austin: State House, 1994.

Bragg, Jefferson Davis. *Louisiana in the Confederacy.* Baton Rouge: Louisiana State University Press, 1941.

Brown, John Henry. *Indian Wars and Pioneers of Texas.* Austin, 1891–92.

Brown, Norman D., ed. *Journey to Pleasant Hill: The Civil War Letters of Captain Elijah P. Petty.* San Antonio: University of Texas Institute of Texan Cultures, 1982.

Buckley, Cornelius Michael. *When Jesuits Were Giants: Louis-Marie Ruellan (1846–1885) and his Contemporaries.* San Francisco: Ignatius, 1999.

Buenger, Walter L. *Secession and the Union in Texas.* Austin: University of Texas Press, 1984.

Castaneda, Carlos E. *Our Catholic Heritage in Texas, 1519–1936.* 7 vols. Austin, 1936.

Cater, Douglas John. *As It Was: Reminiscences of a Soldier of the Third Texas Cavalry in the Civil War.* Introduction by T. Michael Parrish. Austin: State House, 1990.

Chabot, Frederick C. *With the Makers of San Antonio.* San Antonio: Artes Gráficas, 1937.

Chance, Joseph E. *The Second Texas Infantry.* Austin: Eakin, 1984.

Cotham, Edward T., Jr. *Battle on the Bay: The Civil War Struggles for Galveston.* Austin: University of Texas Press, 1998.

Cox, I. Waynne. *The Spanish Acequias of San Antonio.* San Antonio: Maverick, 2005.

Crabb, Martha L. *All Afire to Fight: The Untold Tale of the Civil War's Ninth Texas Cavalry.* New York: Avon Books, 2000.

Current, Richard N., ed. *Encyclopedia of the Confederacy.* 4 vols. New York: Simon & Schuster, 1993.

Cutrer, Thomas W., and T. Michael Parrish. *Brothers in Gray: The Civil War Letters of the Person Family.* Baton Rouge: Louisiana State University Press, 1997.

de la Teja, Jesús F., eds. *A Revolution Remembered: The Memoirs and Selected Correspondence of Juan N. Seguín.* Austin: State House, 1991.

———. *San Antonio de Bèxar: A Community on New Spain's Northern Frontier.* Albuquerque: University of New Mexico Press, 1995.

de Leon, Arnoldo. *The Tejano Community, 1836–1900.* Albuquerque: University of New Mexico Press, 1985.

———. *They Called Them Greasers: Anglo Attitudes toward Mexicans in Texas, 1821–1900.* Austin: University of Texas Press, 1983.

D'Hamel, E. B. *Adventures of a Tenderfoot.* Waco: W. M. Morrison, n.d.

Duganne, Joseph Hickey. *Camps and Prisons: Twenty Months in the Department of the Gulf.* New York: J. P. Robens, 1865.

Dupree, Stephen A. *Planting the Union Flag in Texas: The Campaigns of Major General Nathaniel P. Banks in the West.* College Station: Texas A&M University Press, 2008.

Everett, Donald. E. *San Antonio; The Flavor of Its Past, 1845–1898.* San Antonio: Trinity University Press, 1983.

Falls, Judy, and David Pickering. *Brush Men & Vigilantes: Civil War Dissent in Texas.* College Station: Texas A&M University Press, 2000.

Faulk, Odie B. *General Tom Green: A Fightin' Texas.* Waco: Texian, 1963.

Ford, John Salmon. *Rip Ford's Texas.* Edited by Stephen B. Oates. Austin: University of Texas Press, 1963.

Frazier, Donald. *Blood & Treasure: Confederate Empire in the Southwest.* College Station: Texas A&M University Press, 1995.

———. *Fire in the Cane Field: The Federal Invasion of Louisiana and Texas, January 1861–January 1863.* Buffalo Gap, Tex.: State House, 2009.

Gallaway, B. P. *The Ragged Rebel: A Common Soldier in W. H. Parsons' Texas Cavalry, 1861–1865.* Austin: University of Texas Press, 1988.

———, ed. *Texas: The Dark Corner of the Confederacy.* Norman: University of Oklahoma Press, 1994.

Green, David P. *Place Names of San Antonio, Plus Bexar and Surrounding Counties.* San Antonio: Maverick, 2007.

Hale, Douglas. *The Third Texas Cavalry in the Civil War.* Norman: University of Oklahoma Press, 1993.

Haley, J. Evetts. *Fort Concho and the Texas Frontier.* Midland: Texas Legacy, 2006.

Hall, Martin H. *Confederate Army of New Mexico.* Austin: Presidial, 1978.

———. *Sibley's New Mexico Campaign.* Austin: University of Texas Press, 1960.

Hasskarl, Robert A., and Leif R. Hasskarl. *Waul's Texas Legion, 1862–1865.* Ada, Okla.: Privately printed, 1985.

Hughes, W. J. *Rebellious Ranger: Rip Ford and the Old Southwest.* Norman: University of Oklahoma Press, 1964.

Hunt, Aurora. *The Army of the Pacific.* Glendale, Calif.: Arthur H. Clark, 1951.

———. *Major General James H. Carleton, 1814–1873: Western Frontier Dragoon.* Glendale, Calif.: Arthur H. Clark, 1958.

Johansson, M. Jane. *Peculiar Honor: A History of the 28th Texas Cavalry, 1862–1865.* Fayetteville: University of Arkansas Press, 1998.

Joiner, Gary Dillard. *One Damn Blunder from Beginning to End: The Red River Campaign of 1864*. Wilmington, Del.: Scholarly Resources, 2003.

Lowe, Richard. *Walker's Texas Division, C.S.A.: Greyhounds of the Trans-Mississippi*. Baton Rouge: Louisiana State University Press, 2004.

Marks, Paula Mitchell, ed. *When Will the Weary War Be Over? The Civil War Letters of the Maverick Family of San Antonio*. Dallas: Book Club of Texas, 2008.

Masich, Andrew E. *The Civil War in Arizona: The Story of the California Volunteers, 1861–1865*. Norman: University of Oklahoma Press, 2006.

Matovina, Timothy M. *Tejano Religion and Ethnicity: San Antonio, 1821–1860*. Austin: University of Texas Press, 1995.

McDonald, David R., and Timothy M. Matovina, eds. *Defending Mexican Valor in Texas: Josè Antonio Navarro's Historical Writings, 1853–1857*. Austin: State House, 1995.

McGowen, Stanley S. *Horse Sweat and Powder Smoke: The First Texas Cavalry in the Civil War*. College Station: Texas A&M University Press, 1999.

McGuire, James Patrick. *Iwonski in Texas: Painter and Citizen*. San Antonio: San Antonio Museum Association, 1976.

McIntyre, Benjamin F. *Federals on the Frontier: The Diary of Benjamin F. McIntyre*. Edited by Nannie M. Tilley. Austin: University of Texas Press, 1963.

Miller, Darlis A. *The Confederate Column in New Mexico*. Albuquerque: University of New Mexico Press, 1982.

Montejano, David. *Anglos and Mexicans in the Making of Texas, 1836–1936*. Austin: University of Texas Press, 1987.

Nichols, James L. *The Quartermaster in the Trans-Mississippi*. Austin: University of Texas Press, 1964.

Oates, Stephen B. *Confederate Cavalry West of the River*. Austin: University of Texas Press, 1961.

Pease, S. W. *They Came to San Antonio, 1794–1865*. N.p., n.d.

Pinckney, Pauline A. *Painting in Texas: The Nineteenth Century*. Austin: University of Texas Press, 1967.

Porter, David E. *Incidents and Anecdotes of the Civil War*. Baton Rouge: Louisiana State University Press, 1963.

Poyo, Gerald E., ed. *Tejano Journey, 1770–1850*. Austin: University of Texas Press, 1994.

Ramos, Rául A. *Beyond the Alamo: Forging Mexican Ethnicity in San Antonio, 1821–1861*. Chapel Hill: University of North Carolina Press, 2008.

Reséndez, Andrés. *Changing National Identities at the Frontier: Texas and New Mexico, 1800–1850.* New York: Cambridge University Press, 2005.

Rodríguez, J. M. *Rodríguez Memoirs of Early Texas.* San Antonio, 1961.

Sáenz, Andrés. *Early Tejano Ranching: Daily Life at Ranchos San José & El Fresnillo.* College Station: Texas A&M University Press, 1999.

Schroeder-Lein, Glenna R. *Civil War Medicine.* Armonk, N.Y.: M. E. Sharpe, 2008.

Sibley, Marilyn M. *Lone Stars and State Gazettes: Texas Newspapers before the Civil War.* College Station: Texas A&M University Press, 1983.

Smith, Thomas T. *U.S. Army and the Texas Frontier Economy, 1845–1900.* College Station: Texas A&M University Press, 1999.

Spurlin, Charles D., ed. *Diary of Charles A. Leuschner.* Austin: Eakin, 1992.

Sullivan, Roy. *Civil War in Texas and the Southwest.* Bloomington, Ind.: Author House, 2007.

Thompson, Jerry, ed. *Civil War in the Southwest: Recollections of the Sibley Brigade.* College Station: Texas A&M University Press, 2001.

———. *Confederate General of the West: Henry Hopkins Sibley.* College Station: Texas A&M University Press, 1996.

———, ed. *From Desert to Bayou: The Civil War Journal and Sketches of Morgan Wolfe Merrick.* El Paso: Texas Western, 1991.

———, ed. *Texas and New Mexico on the Eve of the Civil War: The Mansfield & Johnston Inspections, 1859–1861.* Albuquerque: University of New Mexico Press, 2001.

———. *Vaqueros in Blue and Gray.* Austin: State House, 2000.

Thompson, Jerry, and Lawrence T. Jones III. *Civil War and Revolution on the Rio Grande Frontier: A Narrative and Photographic History.* Austin: Texas Historical Association, 2004.

Tijerina, Andrés. *Tejanos & Texas under the Mexican Flag, 1821–1836.* College Station: Texas A&M University Press, 1994.

Townsend, Stephen A. *The Yankee Invasion of Texas.* College Station: Texas A&M University Press, 2006.

Tyler, Ronnie C. *Santiago Vidaurri and the Southern Confederacy.* Austin: Texas State Historical Association, 1973.

War of the Rebellion: A Compilation of the Official Records of the Union and Confederate Armies. 128 vols. Washington, D.C.: Government Printing Office, 1880–1901.

Warner, Ezra J. *Generals in Gray: Lives of the Confederate Commanders.* Baton Rouge: Louisiana State University Press, 1959.

Weber, David J. *The Mexican Frontier, 1821–1846*. Albuquerque: University of New Mexico Press, 1982.

Winsor, Bill. *Texas in the Confederacy: Military Installations, Economy, and People*. Hillsboro, Tex.: Hill College Press, 1978.

Winters, John D. *The Civil War in Louisiana*. Baton Rouge: Louisiana State University Press, 1963.

Wooster, Ralph A., ed. *Civil War Texas*. Austin: Texas State Historical Association, 1999.

———. *Lone Star Blue and Gray*. Austin: Texas State Historical Association, 1995.

———. *Lone Star Generals in Gray*. Austin: Eakin, 2000.

———. *Lone Star Regiments in Gray*. Austin: Eakin, 2002.

———. *Texas and Texans in the Civil War*. Austin: Eakin, 1995.

Wright, Marcus Joseph. *Texas in the War, 1861–1865*. Edited by Harold B. Simpson. Hillsboro, Tex.: Hill College Press, 1965.

ARTICLES AND OTHER PUBLISHED MATERIALS

Austin, Mattie Alice. "The Municipal Government of San Fernando de Béxar, 1730–1800." *Southwestern Historical Quarterly* 8 (April 1905).

Bailey, Anne J. "Thomas James Churchill." In Current, *Encyclopedia of the Confederacy*, 3:311.

———. "Was There a Massacre at Poison Spring?" *Military History of the Southwest* 20 (Fall 1990).

Barr, Alwyn. "The Battle of Blair's Landing." *Louisiana Studies* (Winter 1963).

———. "Texan Losses in the Red River Campaign, 1864." *Texas Military History* (Summer 1963).

———. "Texas Coastal Defense, 1861–1865." *Southwestern Historical Quarterly* 65 (July 1961).

———. "Thomas N. Waul." In Current, *Encyclopedia of the Confederacy*, 4:1695–96.

———. "Tom Green: The Forrest of the Trans-Mississippi." *Louisiana Herald* 88, no. 2.

Brown, Frank W. "The Story of San Antonio Money." *Numismatist* (November 1966).

de la Teja, Jesús F. "Indians, Soldiers, and Canary Islanders: The Making of a Texas Frontier Community." *Locus* (Fall 1990).

———. "Sobrevivencia económica en la frontera de Texas: Los ranchos ganaderos del siglo XVIII en San Antonio de Béxar." *Historia Mexicana* 32 (April–June 1993).

de la Teja, Jesús F., and John Wheat. "Béxar: Profile of a Tejano Community, 1820–1832." *Southwestern Historical Quarterly* 89 (July 1985).

DeWitt, Bart. "Authentic Account of the Death of Ben Milam." *Frontier Times* 12, no. 7.

Faulk, Odie B. "Confederate Hero at Val Verde." *New Mexico Historical Review* (October 1963).

González, José. "Civil War Hispanics: The Other Side of the Story." *Password* (Spring 2007).

Hutchins, Wells A. "The Community Acequia: Its Origin and Development." *Southwestern Historical Quarterly* 31 (January 1928).

James, Vinton L. "Old Times in San Antonio." *Frontier Times* 6 (July 1929).

Legg, Thomas. "Camille J. Polignac." In Current, *Encyclopedia of the Confederacy*, 2:1222–23.

———. "Hamilton P. Bee." In Current, *Encyclopedia of the Confederacy*, 1:151.

———. "Jean Jacques Alfred Alexander Mouton." In Current, *Encyclopedia of the Confederacy*, 3:1092.

———. "William Steele." In Current, *Encyclopedia of the Confederacy*, 4:1538.

McPherson, Hallie M. "The Plan of William McKendree Gwin for a Colony in North Mexico, 1863–1865." *Pacific Historical Review* (December 1933).

Meiners, Fredericka Ann. "Hamilton P. Bee in the Red River Campaign." *Southwestern Historical Quarterly* 78 (July 1974).

Millett, E. B. "When General Green Was Killed." *Confederate Veteran* (September 1916).

O'Neal, Bill. "Civil War Memoirs of Samuel Alonzo Cooke." *Southwestern Historical Quarterly* 74 (April 1971).

Pollard, Charleen Plumly, ed. "Civil War Letters of George W. Allen." *Southwestern Historical Quarterly* 83 (July 1979).

Poyo, Gerald E. "Immigrants and Integration in Late Eighteenth-Century Béxar." In *Tejano Origins in Eighteenth Century San Antonio*. Edited by Poyo and Gilberto M. Hinojosa. Austin: University of Texas Press, 1991.

Spindler, Frank M. "The History of Hempstead and the Formation of Waller County." *Southwestern Historical Quarterly* 61 (April 1956).

Stephenson, Roy R. "Horace Randal." In Current, *Encyclopedia of the Confederacy,* 3:1305.

Valdez, Joyce. "Hispanic Soldiers Played a Notable Role in the Civil War." *Hispanic* (May 2001).

Wooster, Ralph A., ed. "With the Confederate Cavalry in the West: The Civil War Experiences of Isaac Dunbar Affleck." *Southwestern Historical Quarterly* 83 (July 1979).

"Yturri-Edmunds Historic Site." San Antonio Conservation Society, n.d.

UNPUBLISHED MATERIAL

Almaráz, Félix D., Jr. "A French-Flavored Frontier: Catholicism during the Republic of Texas." Paper delivered at the annual meeting of the Texas State Historical Association, San Antonio, Tex., 2007.

Index

Page numbers in *italics* indicate illustrations.